Fifty S

of Gravy

A CHRISTIAN GETS SAUCY!

a cookbook (and a parody)

by Hallee Bridgeman
a.k.a. "Hallee the Homemaker™"

IF YOU LIKE IT HOT, STAY IN THE KITCHEN

Published by
House of Bread Books™

HB HOUSE OF BREAD ™

Fifty Shades
of Gravy

A CHRISTIAN GETS SAUCY!

a cookbook (and a parody)

by Hallee Bridgeman
a.k.a. "Hallee the Homemaker™"

Hallee's Galley book 1

Submitted for your **pleasure**, a cookbook intended to **dominate** ALL of your "**B**ig **D**ang **S**auce **M**aking" (**BDSM**) **desires**.

Rave Reviews for

Fifty Shades of Gravy

"The perfect gift for a submissive housewife!" –

– a homemaker in **ATLANTA JOURNAL**ed

"Made me want to lick it all up!" –

– a guy in **WASHINGTON POST**ed on his blog

"Mouthwatering … Left me wanting more!" –

– someone in **NEW YORK** said a few **TIMES**

"Doing gravy is no longer torture!" –

– a reader in **OHIO DEMOCRAT**ically opined

"Whipped it, beat it, served it up on a platter!" –

– a lady in **L.A POST**ed

TABLE OF CONTENTS

Fifty Shades of Gravy

INTRODUCTION

In my opinion, a good gravy can make an otherwise mediocre meal great while a bad gravy can make an otherwise amazing meal not so memorable. Gravy in its simplest definition is this:

1) some form of fat,

2) mixed with some form of starch,

3) mixed with some form of liquid.

However, some sauces in this book don't require the thickening power of some form of starch. Liquids from cooking meat can actually be thickened into sauce by using the simple reduction method (applying heat until water and liquids have evaporated to form a thicker sauce).

Gravy is first found, historically, in medieval French cookbooks as *gravé*. When meat was prepared on a spit over an open fire, a pan was placed under the roasting meat to collect the drippings. The fat was then skimmed off of these juices, and this was served as a sauce with the meat. This was a rare, bloody sauce. Because the Bible forbids consumption of blood (Leviticus 7:26), during this same time period, Byzantine Christians and Jews were known to prepare a similar sauce, except that they cooked theirs over a high heat and added wine or fish sauce to it then served it as a dipping sauce for chunks of meat or bread.

Over time, these sauces, or *jus*, were improved with the addition of herbs, spices, and different liquids or fats as well as different thickening agents. Now, as you can tell by this cookbook containing 50 distinct gravy recipes, the disparate preparations and combinations could be considered countless. There are two really simple things you can do to ensure you serve the best gravy possible.

First, always use fresh, real, whole foods. It is painfully obvious when gravy comes "fresh" out of a jar or a magical "just add water" packet of dehydrated chemicals. The fact is you just can't beat the taste of homemade, fresh, real, whole foods. Don't let clever marketing gurus fool you into thinking a jar or packet is going to be the same or better. There's simply no way something packaged with industrial grade chemical additives and preservatives in a modern factory can ever compete with a product made from scratch in your very own kitchen with simple whole food ingredients and *love*.

Second, taste it – a lot. That's right. "Stick it and lick it" Plain, bland, boring gravy can kill a meal. You must taste it the entire time you're preparing it. as in stick a clean spoon into the sauce and lick it off to see if the taste suits. Whenever I volunteer in the soup kitchen, I keep a ready supply of clean plastic spoons in my apron pocket. I "stick and lick" and dispose of those spoons the entire time I cook. The drippings and pan scrapings from preparing meats will never taste the same twice. You must use your senses – smell and look and taste – and add flavor enhancing herbs and spices as needed.

Some of the recipes you will find are entire meals (like Family Favorite Steak & Gravy), some are simple sauces (Au Jus), and some are gravies you make to serve alongside your prepared feast (Traditional Turkey Gravy). There are meaty gravies, comfort food gravies, vegan gravies, gluten-free gravies, and even chocolate gravies. Serve them over biscuits, rice, mashed potatoes, toast, sides, entrees, or simply lick the spoon and savor that liquid comfort we call gravy. Enjoy them.

HOW TO READ THIS COOKBOOK

You will find symbols at the top of each recipe to help you better use and navigate this cookbook. Here is a key (legend) to assist you in interpreting them.

       Freezes well

Sometimes, it's nice to pre-make something, or make big batches and freeze the quantity you'll need. You can just pull a container out of the freezer and gravy is ready to go when you need it. For the broths and stocks, I freeze in 1-cup increments. For gravies, freeze and re-heat to 165°, whisking it smooth.

       Quick and Easy

Some nights or mornings, quick and easy is the theme of the meal. These gravies take little preparation and use supplies that don't take a lot of preparation or cooking times.

       Lent/Daniel Fast/Vegan Friendly

These dishes are 100% real whole food, vegan friendly. No meat products, no meat, no dairy or egg, no processed foods. Suitable for a Daniel Fast, Lent, or incorporating into a vegan menu.

       Vegetarian

Not "vegan" – may contain dairy products or egg, but no meat.

       Kosher Friendly

If you keep Kosher, your kitchen is Kosher, and your ingredients are Kosher, these dishes are Kosher friendly. No dairy mixing with meat, no unclean meats, etc.

       Holiday Fare

This dish goes well with a roast turkey, rack of lamb, goose, or a roast beef: traditional holiday meals.

Gluten Free

All ingredients in this recipe are gluten free.

   International

A recipe that is a traditional dish in a country other than the United States.

   Calls for alcohol

This recipe originally calls for alcohol, usually wine. If you abstain from alcohol even in cooking, in that case you can substitute a 100% pure white or dark grape juice (make sure there is no apple juice in it) along with one teaspoon of distilled vinegar to approximate the same flavor and properties while cooking but without the alcohol.

   Crock Pot

Either can be or should be prepared in a crock pot. It's wonderful to have a dish you can leave cooking on its own while you do your day.

   Entrée

This is not "just" a gravy - it is a full entrée.

Other symbols used in this cookbook:

   More information on the world wide web

When you can find more information about something on the internet, I have put an INFORMATION symbol ⓘ next to it and provided the link address in the notes.

YOU ARE WHAT YOU EAT: INGREDIENTS

While the title and introduction of this book are fun and a parody, the recipes are absolutely real (well, except maybe for the fun titles). I find no greater way to show my love to my friends and family than to provide them with amazing food created with good ingredients. There are three main principles I follow in cooking:

1. Eat only substances God created for food. Avoid what is not designed for food.

2. As much as possible, eat foods as they were created – before they were changed or converted into something humans think might be better

3. Avoid food addictions. Let no food or drink become your god.

In keeping with these three principles, almost everything I cook is made from scratch. While this notion may sound odd to modern readers, cooking with fresh, whole, organically and locally grown food was common and normal until as recently as 25 years ago.

If a recipe calls for broth, I have frozen broth on hand that I've made from scratch from a raw stock at some point in the recent past. In the beginning of the recipes section a few pages from here, you'll find recipes for hearty beef broth, rich turkey broth, savory chicken broth, and healthy vegetable broth. Feel free to use these recipes whenever this cookbook (or any other) calls for stock or broth.

If you don't happen to make your own stocks or broth, you can substitute canned or prepackaged stock or broth. One thing to be wary of when purchasing anything like broth, bouillon, or stock, is to watch out for monosodium glutamate or MSG. MSG is a food preservative that is actually a neurotoxin, and many people have adverse reactions to it – yet it is found in MANY prepackaged and processed foods … especially bouillon and broth products.

Whenever milk is called for in a recipe, I use whole milk ⓘ. I don't cook with milk that has lower fat content than whole. If you do, you may need to adjust your recipe accordingly.

Whenever I refer to butter, I am talking about actual butter, not substitutes. Butter should be unsalted, real butter. I do not cook with salted butter or any kind of margarine or "buttery spread".

I do my best to avoid genetically modified foods (GMOs). Topping the list of GMOs are corn, soy, and canola. This is why, when a recipe calls for corn starch, I always recommend using organic corn starch. If you can't find organic corn starch in your area, you can also use arrowroot starch or tapioca starch though either will taste a bit sweeter than corn starch.

I almost exclusively use extra virgin olive oil in my cooking. At time of print for this cookbook, organic canola oil is incredibly expensive. Generically labeled "vegetable oil" is almost always genetically modified (GMO) corn oil or processed soy oil. Any kind of processed soy ⓘ, even from organic soy bean, is <u>very toxic to men and boys</u> and not really recommended for females either!

On my Hallee the Homemaker website, I list the "Dirty Dozen ⓘ" – that is, the top GMO foods and the foods you should always try to purchase as certified organic if you don't grow your own or have access to a trusted sustainable local farm.

The "Dirty Dozen" foods that are the most contaminated on average are:

1 Peaches	5 Nectarines	9 Grapes (imported)
2 Apples	6 Strawberries	10 Pears
3 Sweet Bell Peppers	7 Cherries	11 Spinach
4 Celery	8 Lettuce	12 Potatoes

In my kitchen, I personally grind organic wheat or corn to make my own flour or corn meal. If you also have a grain mill, I use fresh-ground organic soft white wheat. Most recipes in this book use flour as a thickening agent. If you don't have your own mill, I recommend substituting organic whole wheat flour. Note that fresh-ground flour is not the same as even organic whole wheat flour from a grocery store shelf. Store-bought whole wheat flour will not act exactly the same, and any white flour is incredibly bad for human health – essentially transforming instantly into sugar when eaten. So, experiment with different whole wheat flours and see what works and what doesn't work for you. The amount needed in the recipes is nominal and can easily be adjusted.

Probably the biggest thing you'll notice throughout this cookbook is that I never cook with pork. My family follows a Levitical Diet ⓘ – in that we don't eat foods that are specifically prohibited by the Bible. This means pork and bottom feeders like catfish and all shellfish are out. The truth is we don't miss pork in our diet. Turkey breakfast sausage is a favorite in our home. Turkey ham is a substitute that works in moderation for ham. And beef bacon is amazing and wonderfully versatile - as well as better tasting than any pork bacon any of us ever tasted.

ⓘ For more information on the world wide web, visit:

http://www.halleethehomemaker.com/2011/04/the-dirty-dozen/

http://www.halleethehomemaker.com/levitical-diet/

http://www.halleethehomemaker.com/2009/09/soy-oh-boy/

http://www.halleethehomemaker.com/2012/10/milk-it-does-a-body-good/

FREE INDEED

We live in a world that groans beneath the weight of sin that entered at the fall of man. Everywhere we turn, there is pain, hatred, abuse, war, jealousy, greed, and malice. Whether they consciously do it or not, people seeking to free themselves from their chains, longing to end their internal suffering, turn to all types of carnality. They are lost in a world that offers them, not truth, but lies.

The Biblical book of Galatians spells out the types of gratification of the flesh lost people seek when they ache for peace and freedom: adultery, fornication, uncleanness, lewdness ... yet even when carnally fulfilled, human souls still cry out for freedom from the ropes that bind and enslave us to our sin.

This cookbook is a purposeful parody of a piece of fiction that glorifies the kind of unbalanced dominance and submission that leads to pain, abandonment, forced (non-consensual) sexual acts, and brokenness. While it is a parody, the very serious and very real fact is that there are real people all around us who desperately seek tranquility and truth in this world and who, instead, fall into the trap of pain and bondage in the vain hope that suffering will fulfill their quest. The world promises that a total surrender to the pleasure/pain promised by the flesh will free us, but the Bible warns us that such will only further trap us.

The good news is that Christ can free us from all of our bonds. He is the Bread of Life. Accepting Christ into our lives brings with it the Holy Spirit, and the Spirit brings us love, joy, peace, patience, kindness, goodness, faithfulness, gentleness, and self-control.

When we embrace the love of Christ, we break the chains of slavery to heartache, pain, and sin. We open our hearts and lives to enduring unconditional love and lasting peace.

"Jesus answered them, 'Most assuredly, I say to you, whoever commits sin is a slave of sin. And a slave does not abide in the house forever, but a son abides forever. Therefore if the Son makes you free, you shall be free indeed.'" John 8:34.

STURDY STOCKS & BESTED BROTHS

Many people assume that the words "stock" and "broth" are simply interchangeable terms for the same thing: a liquid naturally flavored with vegetables, meat, and/or bones that is often used as the base for soups, sauces, gravies, and other dishes. Actually, there is a slight but significant difference, though this significance is fairly confined to the culinary world. In any American grocery store, you will definitely see "stock" and "broth" used as synonyms to describe the same product.

Raw stock is intended to be used as a base to make other things like soups, sauces, braises, risottos, or gravies. Stock is technically what is made when you simmer vegetables and aromatics – or vegetables and aromatics with meat scraps and bones – in order to extract their flavor. Traditionally, there's no salt and none of the many other seasonings modern cooks use to enhance the flavor. Skimming while heating, then draining off all solids and fats, results in a savory raw stock. Raw stock isn't meant to be eaten on its own. In fact, stock doesn't really even taste all that good. Raw stock by itself can taste muted, flat, and overly vegetal or meaty.

Broth, on the other hand, is something that can be eaten on its own. A good definition for broth would be "seasoned stock." With the possible addition of salt and other seasonings, fats, or thickening agents, broth is tasty and satisfying.

It might seem like stock will always end up salted and seasoned whenever it is used, so saying there's a significant difference between the two is just splitting hairs. But the point of stock is that you have control over how it gets salted and seasoned. It's a blank slate, the base or foundation to build all the flavors upon, and an already-seasoned broth is not.

For example, if the stock is to be reduced down to a sauce, starting off with a salted broth could make the reduction taste far too salty. If the stock is to be used for poaching fish, you only want a little or no salt, so you would definitely want a light vegetable stock instead of a salted broth.

When making either, remember that the vegetables need not be absolutely fresh. In fact, making stocks regularly is a great way to clean out the pantry shelves and crisper drawers to use up all your supplies without waste. Slightly wilted celery or carrots and somewhat dry onions or garlic cloves, or those barely wrinkled potatoes that are just starting to sprout may not be something you would serve up at a Sunday potluck – but all of them make a perfectly fine stock provided they aren't actually spoiled. Remember, too, that if you make a salt free vegetable stock, you can put the solids right onto your compost pile.

STOCKY VEGETABLE BROTH

Make this vegetable broth and freeze it in 1-cup increments. I use breast milk storage bags ① to freeze my broth. They are sterile, freezer safe, the perfect size, and have measurement marks right on them like a measuring cup. Then, when you need beef broth or beef stock, just pull it out of the freezer and defrost it.

INGREDIENTS:

For a stock, you will only need:

1 TBS extra virgin olive oil
1 large onion
2 stalks celery, including the leaves
2 large carrots
1 bunch green onions
8 cloves garlic
8 sprigs fresh parsley
6 sprigs fresh thyme
2 bay leaves
2 quarts water

If you are making a broth, add:

salt and pepper to taste (Kosher or sea salt is best/fresh ground pepper is best) and other herbs and seasonings of choice to taste

SUPPLIES:

Sharp knife/cutting board
Saucepan with lid or crock pot
Measuring cups/spoons
Mesh strainer

PREPARATION:

Peel then roughly chop the carrots.
Halve the garlic.
Roughly chop the celery.
Quarter the onion

DIRECTIONS:

Place all of the ingredients in a crock pot and cook on low for 6 hours, skimming occasionally.

-OR-

Place all of the ingredients in the saucepan. Bring to a boil. Reduce heat. Cover and simmer on low for several hours, skimming occasionally.

Strain the solids from the stock with the mesh strainer.

Freeze.

YIELD:

8 cups

NUTRITION:

Nutrition Facts

Serving Size 61 g

Amount Per Serving

Calories 43	Calories from Fat 18

% Daily Value*

Total Fat 2.0g	3%
Trans Fat 0.0g	
Cholesterol 0mg	0%
Sodium 311mg	13%
Total Carbohydrates 6.4g	2%
Dietary Fiber 1.7g	7%
Sugars 2.1g	
Protein 1.0g	

Vitamin A 66%	•	Vitamin C 13%	
Calcium 5%	•	Iron 9%	

No cholesterol

High in calcium

High in dietary fiber

High in iron

High in manganese

High in potassium

Very high in vitamin A

High in vitamin B6

Very high in vitamin C

NOTES:

If you are making a broth, each time you skim, sample the liquid and add salt, pepper, and any other herbs and spices you like to taste. Remember that Kosher or sea salt is best. Iodized salt can add too much iodine to the mixture. Fresh ground pepper is always best.

Use in any recipe that calls for vegetable broth or vegetable stock.

ⓘ For information about freezing in breast milk bags, check out this link: http://www.halleethehomemaker.com/2010/05/the-perfect-solution-for-freezing-broth/

STOCKY BEEF BROTH

Make this beef broth and freeze it in 1-cup increments. I use breast milk storage bags ① to freeze my broth. They are sterile, freezer safe, the perfect size, and have measurement marks right on them like a measuring cup. Whenever you need beef broth or beef stock, just pull it out of the freezer and defrost it.

 INGREDIENTS:

For a stock, you will only need:
1 large beef soup bone -AND/OR- 1 pound beef trimmings (whatever you have on hand)
6 cups filtered water
3 carrots
2 celery ribs (with leaves)
1 small onion
4 medium fresh white mushrooms
2 small bay leaves
1 tsp dried parsley
1 pinch ground thyme
1/2 tsp garlic powder
1/4 tsp paprika
1 TBS gluten-free soy sauce

If you are making a broth, add:
salt and pepper to taste (Kosher or sea salt is best/fresh ground pepper is best) and other herbs and seasonings of choice to taste

 SUPPLIES:
Sharp knife/cutting board
Saucepan with lid or crock pot
Measuring cups/spoons
Mesh strainer

 PREPARATION:
Peel then roughly chop the carrots.
Roughly chop the celery.
Quarter the onion
Halve the mushrooms

DIRECTIONS:

Place all of the ingredients in a crock pot and cook on low for 6 hours, skimming occasionally.

-OR-

Place all of the ingredients in the saucepan. Bring to a boil. Reduce heat. Cover and simmer on low for several hours, skimming occasionally.

Strain the solids from the stock with the mesh strainer.

Freeze.

YIELD:

6 cups

NUTRITION:

Nutrition Facts		
Serving Size 155 g		
Amount Per Serving		
Calories 136		Calories from Fat 45
		% Daily Value*
Total Fat 5.0g		8%
Saturated Fat 2.1g		10%
Trans Fat 0.0g		
Cholesterol 41mg		14%
Sodium 447mg		19%
Total Carbohydrates 6.0g		2%
Dietary Fiber 1.8g		7%
Sugars 2.6g		
Protein 17.4g		
Vitamin A 106%	•	Vitamin C 7%
Calcium 3%	•	Iron 16%

High in iron

Very high in vitamin A

Very high in vitamin B6

NOTES:

If you are making a broth, each time you skim, sample the liquid and add salt, pepper, and any other herbs and spices you like to taste. Remember that Kosher or sea salt is best. Iodized salt can add too much iodine to the mixture. Fresh ground pepper is always best.

ⓘ For information about freezing in breast milk bags, check out this link: http://www.halleethehomemaker.com/2010/05/the-perfect-solution-for-freezing-broth/

DON'T BE A CHICKEN STALKER CHICKEN BROTH

STOCKY CHICKEN BROTH

Make this chicken broth and freeze it in 1-cup increments. I use breast milk storage bags ⓘ to freeze my broth. They are sterile, freezer safe, the perfect size, and have measurement marks right on them like a measuring cup. Then, when you need chicken stock or broth, just pull it out of the freezer and defrost it.

INGREDIENTS:

For a stock, you will only need:
2 $^1/_2$ pounds bony chicken pieces (in other words, the bones, meat bits, skin, any part of the bird you don't care to eat)
8 cups filtered water
2 celery ribs with leaves
2 carrots
2 medium onions
2 bay leaves
$^1/_2$ teaspoon dried rosemary, crushed
$^1/_2$ teaspoon dried thyme
8 to 10 whole peppercorns

If you are making a broth, add:
salt and pepper to taste (Kosher or sea salt is best/fresh ground pepper is best) and other herbs and seasonings of choice to taste

SUPPLIES:
Sharp knife/cutting board
Saucepan with lid or crock pot
Measuring cups/spoons
Mesh strainer

PREPARATION:
Peel then roughly chop the carrots.
Roughly chop the celery.
Quarter the onion

DIRECTIONS:
Place all of the ingredients in a crock pot and cook on low for 6 hours, skimming occasionally.

-OR-

Place all of the ingredients in the saucepan. Bring to a boil. Reduce heat. Cover and simmer on low for several hours, skimming occasionally.

Strain the solids from the stock with the mesh strainer.

Freeze.

 YIELD:

6 cups

 NUTRITION:

Nutrition Facts	
Serving Size 267 g	
Amount Per Serving	
Calories 314	Calories from Fat 53
	% Daily Value*
Total Fat 5.9g	9%
Saturated Fat 1.7g	8%
Trans Fat 0.0g	
Cholesterol 146mg	49%
Sodium 151mg	6%
Total Carbohydrates 7.0g	2%
Dietary Fiber 1.8g	7%
Sugars 2.8g	
Protein 55.7g	
Vitamin A 70% •	Vitamin C 10%
Calcium 5% •	Iron 12%

Low in sodium

Very high in niacin

Very high in selenium

Very high in vitamin A

High in phosphorus

High in vitamin B6

 NOTES:

If you are making a broth, each time you skim, sample the liquid and add salt, pepper, and any other herbs and spices you like to taste. Remember that Kosher or sea salt is best. Iodized salt can add too much iodine to the mixture. Fresh ground pepper is always best.

If your family regularly eats rotisserie chickens, after the meal, break up the carcasses to reduce their size and store them in the freezer until you have collected three or four carcasses. That is enough bone and meat to make a great chicken stock. Another option is to talk to your local butcher or even your grocery store butcher shop about purchasing just scraps like the wing tips and necks, in bulk at a discount.

Use in any recipe that calls for chicken broth or chicken stock.

ⓘ For information about freezing in breast milk bags, check out this link: http://www.halleethehomemaker.com/2010/05/the-perfect-solution-for-freezing-broth/

STOCKY TURKEY BROTH

Make this turkey broth and freeze it in 1-cup increments. I use breast milk storage bags ⓘ to freeze my broth. They are sterile, freezer safe, the perfect size, and have measurement marks right on them like a measuring cup. Then, when you need turkey stock or broth, just pull it out of the freezer and defrost it.

INGREDIENTS:

For a stock, you will only need:
1 turkey carcass, need not be intact
turkey skin and any remaining giblets (in other words, the bones, meat bits, skin, any part of the bird you don't care to eat)
2 cups dry white wine ⓘ
6 cloves garlic
4 stalks of celery, with leaves
4 carrots
3 onions
2 tsp Kosher or sea salt
1 TBS whole black peppercorns
water to cover
$\frac{1}{2}$ tsp basil
$\frac{1}{2}$ tsp parsley

If you are making a broth, add:
salt and pepper to taste (Kosher or sea salt is best/fresh ground pepper is best) and other herbs and seasonings of choice to taste

SUPPLIES:
Sharp knife/cutting board
Saucepan with lid or crock pot
Measuring cups/spoons
Mesh strainer

PREPARATION:
Peel then roughly chop the carrots.
Halve the garlic.
Roughly chop the celery.
Quarter the onion

DIRECTIONS:

Place all of the ingredients in the crock pot and cook on low for 6 hours.

-OR-

Place all of the ingredients in the saucepan. Bring to a boil. Cover and simmer on low for several hours.

Strain the broth with the mesh strainer.

Freeze.

YIELD:

6 quarts

NUTRITION:

Nutrition Facts

Serving Size 69 g

Amount Per Serving

Calories 27	Calories from Fat 3
	% Daily Value
Total Fat 0.3g	**0%**
Trans Fat 0.0g	
Cholesterol 3mg	**1%**
Sodium 77mg	**3%**
Total Carbohydrates 3.5g	**1%**
Dietary Fiber 0.5g	**2%**
Sugars 0.7g	
Protein 1.5g	

Vitamin A 13%	•	Vitamin C 1%
Calcium 1%	•	Iron 2%

Very high in vitamin A

High in selenium

Low in saturated fat

NOTES:

If you are making a broth, each time you skim, sample the liquid and add salt, pepper, and any other herbs and spices you like to taste. Fresh ground pepper is always best. Kosher or sea salt is best. Iodized salt can add too much iodine to the mixture. Use in any recipe that calls for turkey broth or turkey stock.

ⓘ For information about freezing in breast milk bags, check out this link: http://www.halleethehomemaker.com/2010/05/the-perfect-solution-for-freezing-broth/

ⓘ If you abstain from alcohol even in cooking, you can substitute a 100% pure grape juice (ensure there is no apple juice in it) and one teaspoon of distilled vinegar to approximate the same flavor and properties while cooking.

INTRODUCTION TO BEEF GRAVY

In western culture, gravy is liquid comfort. Gravy is even part of our vernacular, so much so that we want to ride the gravy train, have everything come up gravy, and get enough done so that the rest is all just gravy.

In researching to write this cookbook, I came across a lot of really interesting facts. For example, many of the snobbiest chefs on earth are of a mind that a recipe for gravy is overkill. For example, Hugh Fearnley-Whittingstall writes in his River Cottage Meat Book, "there is no recipe for gravy, nor should there be." And I guess that's true if you're a world famous chef but I really like recipes.

Another interesting fact I discovered is that there is no French translation for gravy. The closest words to it don't even sound right. I can't imagine any kind of train being powered by *effete jus* or everything coming up *sauce brune*. In French cuisine, there are basically two main schools of gravy making: roux and deglaze.

Adding flour to the fatty drippings and juices produced as a byproduct of cooking the meat makes a roux. The flour is added right into the pan where the drippings reside. The result is a roux, a thickening agent made of flour and fat, that is a base for a gravy. For the deglazers, they simply deglaze the pan with alcohol, usually a hearty wine, or some raw stock and a little vinegar, before adding more liquid to make the gravy or sauce.

Gravy, the types of gravy, the means of making gravy, and the flavor enhancement that gravy brings to your entrees and sides differs with every meal. This section focusing on beef gravy begins with probably the simplest gravy there is, the French *au jus*. While in modern times, an *au jus* is considered more of a dip or a sauce, historically, it is the very earliest form of gravy.

The *au jus* is closely followed by a horseradish gravy that also contains a really good steak sauce recipe. The remainder of the section are some popular and easy beef based recipes to get you started.

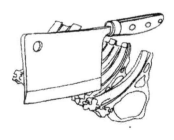

AU JUS (French Dip)

French dip is one of my favorite sandwiches. Thinly sliced roast beef, caramelized onions, roasted peppers, creamy provolone cheese on sourdough bread – then, dipped into a flavorful *au jus*.
This dip is *good*.

 INGREDIENTS:

$^1/_4$ cup fat from roast beef drippings

1 $^1/_2$ TBS flour (I use fresh ground soft white wheat)

2 cups beef broth

Salt and pepper to taste (Kosher or sea salt is best/fresh ground pepper is best)

 SUPPLIES:

Saucepan

Whisk

Measuring cups/spoons

 PREPARATION:

Prepare the roast beef. OR – save the drippings from a roast in the refrigerator or freezer.

 DIRECTIONS:

Melt the fat in the pan over medium-high heat. Whisk in the flour. Cook, whisking constantly, until it thickens. Whisk in the broth. Stir with whisk until smooth. Bring to a boil and stir until it thickens slightly. Add salt and pepper to taste.

 YIELD:

4 servings

NUTRITION:

Nutrition Facts	
Serving Size 136 g	
Amount Per Serving	
Calories 145	Calories from Fat 122
	% Daily Value*
Total Fat 13.5g	21%
Saturated Fat 6.6g	33%
Cholesterol 14mg	5%
Sodium 382mg	16%
Total Carbohydrates 2.7g	1%
Protein 2.7g	
Vitamin A 0% • Vitamin C 0%	
Calcium 1% • Iron 2%	

Very low in sugar

NOTES:

Serve with prime rib or French Dip sandwiches.

Salt and pepper taste will change depending on the flavor of the beef drippings.

HORSERADISH GRAVY
(AND BONUS STEAK SAUCE RECIPE)

We have a horseradish plant that grows out of control in our yard. I'm always on the lookout for reasons to use horseradish. This is DE-LICIOUS over a grilled steak.

INGREDIENTS:

To Make Steak Sauce:

1 cup ketchup
$^1/_2$ cup onion, coarsely chopped ①
1 large clove garlic
$^1/_4$ cup water
$^1/_4$ cup Worcestershire sauce
$^1/_4$ cup lemon juice
$^1/_4$ cup white vinegar
2 tablespoons soy sauce
2 tablespoons brown sugar
1 tablespoons prepared mustard

To Make This Gravy Recipe:

1 $^1/_2$ cups beef broth
$^1/_2$ cup steak sauce
1 TBS horseradish
2 tsp flour (I use fresh-ground soft white wheat)
Salt and pepper to taste (Kosher or sea salt is best/fresh ground pepper is best)

SUPPLIES:

To Make Steak Sauce:

Saucepan
Sharp knife/cutting board
Measuring cups/spoons
Spoon
Strainer

To Make This Gravy Recipe:

Saucepan
Measuring cups/spoons
Small bowl/whisk

PREPARATION:

Prepare steak sauce: Mix all ingredients in saucepan. Heat to boiling. Reduce heat and simmer for 30 minutes, stirring occasionally. Strain. Store in refrigerator for up to two weeks.

Finely chop horseradish.

DIRECTIONS:

Combine 1 cup of the beef broth, steak sauce, and horseradish in saucepan. Heat to boiling.

Whisk together remaining $^1/_2$ cup of the beef broth with the flour. Whisk into the boiling liquid in the pan. Reduce heat and simmer for 5 minutes.

Salt and pepper to taste.

YIELD:

8 servings

NUTRITION:

Nutrition Facts

Serving Size 62 g

Amount Per Serving	
Calories 23	Calories from Fat 3
	% Daily Value*
Total Fat 0.3g	0%
Cholesterol 0mg	0%
Sodium 382mg	16%
Total Carbohydrates 3.4g	1%
Sugars 1.9g	
Protein 1.0g	
Vitamin A 0% •	Vitamin C 1%
Calcium 0% •	Iron 1%

Low in saturated fat

No cholesterol

High in niacin

NOTES:

Delicious served with steak or roast beef.

ⓘ For information about a tip for chopping onions, follow this link: http://www.halleethehomemaker.com/chopping-veg/

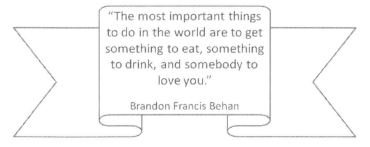

"The most important things to do in the world are to get something to eat, something to drink, and somebody to love you."

Brandon Francis Behan

BEEF GRAVY MIX

Sometimes, it's handy to have the ability to make a quick gravy. If you are careful with ingredients (watch for MSG), this is a great product to have on-hand in those time-crunch moments.

INGREDIENTS:
1 cup dry milk
$^1/_2$ cup flour (I use fresh-ground soft white wheat)
2 TBS instant beef bouillon granules (no MSG)
1 $^1/_2$ tsp dried thyme
1 tsp dried rosemary
$^1/_2$ tsp dried sage
$^1/_2$ tsp fresh ground black pepper
$^1/_2$ cup unsalted butter
1 TBS browning sauce for gravy (no MSG)

SUPPLIES:
Small bowl with cover
Fork

PREPARATION:
Crush the thyme and rosemary

DIRECTIONS:
In a small bowl, stir together the milk, flour, bouillon, spices, and pepper. Using the fork, cut the butter in until completely blended. Stir in the browning sauce.

Cover and refrigerate for up to 6 weeks.

To make gravy:

Pour 1 cup cold water into a saucepan. Whisk in $^1/_2$ cup of the gravy mix. Bring to a boil. Reduce heat and cook, stirring constantly, for 3 minutes.

YIELD:
3 cups of mix makes 6 batches of 4-servings gravy (for a total of 24 servings)

NUTRITION:

Nutrition Facts

Serving Size 21 g

Amount Per Serving	
Calories 54	Calories from Fat 38
	% Daily Value*
Total Fat 4.2g	6%
Saturated Fat 2.6g	13%
Trans Fat 0.0g	
Cholesterol 11mg	4%
Sodium 610mg	25%
Total Carbohydrates 3.2g	1%
Sugars 0.7g	
Protein 0.9g	
Vitamin A 2% •	Vitamin C 0%
Calcium 0% •	Iron 1%

High in vitamin B6

Very high in vitamin B12

NOTES:

You can freeze this and keep it longer than 6 weeks. Freeze $^1/_2$ cups at a time in freezer bags with instructions for preparation written on the outside of the bag. It will keep for several months that way.

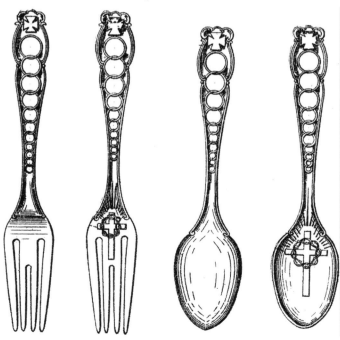

BEEF BACON GRAVY

Whenever I'm serving biscuits with beef bacon, I always make a batch of gravy to go with them. It is the perfect compliment to a big country breakfast – especially when you're having breakfast for dinner.

INGREDIENTS:

12-ounces beef bacon (smoked & cured beef plate)
$^1/_4$ cup flour (I use fresh ground soft white wheat)
2 cups milk
1 tsp salt (Kosher or sea salt is best)
$^1/_2$ tsp fresh ground pepper

SUPPLIES:

Skillet
Measuring cups/spoons
Paper towel lined plate
Whisk
Fork or tongs

PREPARATION:

Fry the bacon in the skillet until browned and crisp. Remove from the pan and drain on the paper towel lined plate.

DIRECTIONS:

Sprinkle the flour into the bacon grease remaining in the pan. Using the whisk, whisk until smooth.

Slowly whisk in the milk. Bring to a boil over medium heat, regularly stirring the mixture. Boil and stir for 2 minutes.

Add the salt and pepper to taste.

YIELD:

8 servings

NUTRITION:

Nutrition Facts

Serving Size 108 g

Amount Per Serving	
Calories 111	Calories from Fat 53
	% Daily Value*
Total Fat 5.9g	9%
Saturated Fat 3.6g	18%
Trans Fat 0.0g	
Cholesterol 24mg	8%
Sodium 597mg	25%
Total Carbohydrates 5.9g	2%
Sugars 3.1g	
Protein 6.2g	
Vitamin A 0% •	Vitamin C 0%
Calcium 1% •	Iron 5%

Very high in vitamin B6

Very high in vitamin B12

NOTES:

Serve over biscuits, ① or fried potatoes ①.

I don't always make beef bacon gravy when I make beef bacon, so I store the grease in a jar in the refrigerator. When I want to make gravy from it, I'll scoop out $1/4$ cup of the grease and melt it in the skillet before proceeding with the rest of the instructions.

① For Hallee the Homemaker's Whole Wheat Buttermilk Biscuits, check out this link:
http://www.halleethehomemaker.com/buttermilk-biscuits/

① For Hallee the Homemaker's Family Fit Fried Potatoes recipe, check out this link:
http://www.halleethehomemaker.com/skillet-taters/

PROVOCATIVELY QUICK & SHAMEFULLY EASY HANDCUFFED
HAMBURGER GRAVY

QUICK & EASY HAMBURGER GRAVY

I have made this so many times. It's a nice "I need something quick but satisfying for dinner" kind of dish. It whips up in no time and is wonderful served over mashed potatoes or rice.

INGREDIENTS:
1 lb grass fed ground beef
1 small onion
1 tsp salt (Kosher or sea salt is best)
$^{1}/_{2}$ tsp fresh ground pepper
$^{1}/_{2}$ tsp garlic powder
1 cup beef broth
2 TBS flour (I use fresh ground soft white wheat)

SUPPLIES:
Skillet
Sharp knife/cutting board
Measuring cups/spoons
Jar with a lid

PREPARATION:
Chop the onion ①.

DIRECTIONS:
Crumble the beef into the skillet. Add the onion. Heat over medium-high heat until the beef is browned. Season with the garlic, salt, and pepper.

Put the flour and the broth into the jar. Cover and shake until well blended. Slowly stir into the beef mixture.

Cook, stirring, until mixture thickens and boils. Boil and stir for 2 minutes.

YIELD:
4 servings

NUTRITION:

Nutrition Facts	
Serving Size 197 g	
Amount Per Serving	
Calories 233	Calories from Fat 103
	% Daily Value*
Total Fat 11.4g	18%
Saturated Fat 4.6g	23%
Cholesterol 75mg	25%
Sodium 848mg	35%
Total Carbohydrates 5.3g	2%
Dietary Fiber 0.5g	2%
Sugars 1.0g	
Protein 25.0g	
Vitamin A 0% • Vitamin C 2%	
Calcium 3% • Iron 18%	

Low in sugar

High in iron

NOTES:

Serve as a main dish over mashed potatoes.

ⓘ For Hallee the Homemaker's Wonderful Whipped Potatoes recipe, check out this link:
http://www.halleethehomemaker.com/whipped-potatoes/

ⓘ For Hallee the Homemaker's Perfect Brown Rice recipe, check out this link:
http://www.halleethehomemaker.com/brown-rice/

ⓘ For Hallee the Homemaker's Perfect White Rice recipe, check out this link:
http://www.halleethehomemaker.com/white-rice/

ⓘ For information about a tip for chopping onions, follow this link:
http://www.halleethehomemaker.com/chopping-veg/

SAUCE ON A SLICE

This is a dish my retired Sergeant Major dad often fondly talks of his mother preparing for him. In the original name, the first "S" in the title did not stand for "Sauce" and the second "S" stood for "Shingle." But, I want to keep my PG rating, so we're taking artistic license and renaming it.

INGREDIENTS:

2-ounce package dried beef (read package and avoid MSG)
$1/4$ cup unsalted butter
$1/4$ cup flour (I use fresh ground soft white wheat)
2 cups whole milk
$1/4$ tsp fresh ground pepper
4 slices of bread

SUPPLIES:

Sharp knife/cutting board
Skillet
Measuring cups/spoons
Whisk

PREPARATION:

Toast bread.
Slice beef into thin ribbons.

DIRECTIONS:

Melt the butter in the skillet over medium heat. Whisk in the flour until smooth. Slowly whisk in the milk. Heat over medium heat until it thickens and boils. Cook for 2 minutes.

Stir in the pepper and the beef.

Serve over the toast.

YIELD:

4 servings

NUTRITION:

Nutrition Facts		
Serving Size 167 g		
Amount Per Serving		
Calories 254		Calories from Fat 151
		% Daily Value*
Total Fat 16.7g		26%
Saturated Fat 10.0g		50%
Cholesterol 55mg		18%
Sodium 201mg		8%
Total Carbohydrates 16.1g		5%
Sugars 6.8g		
Protein 9.9g		
Vitamin A 10%	•	Vitamin C 0%
Calcium 16%	•	Iron 7%

High in calcium

High in vitamin A

NOTES:

This goes just as nicely over fried potatoes as it does over bread. It could still be S.O.S., but maybe called "Sauce on Shingles".

ⓘ For Hallee the Homemaker's Family Fit Fried Potatoes recipe, check out this link:

http://www.halleethehomemaker.com/skillet-taters/

QUICK & EASY BEEF GRAVY

This is a great recipe to have on hand when you need to finish up a meal with a quick gravy. It would go well with meat loaf or steak or even a roast beef if you end up without drippings in a pan.

INGREDIENTS:

2 TBS unsalted butter
1 $^1/_2$ tsp extra virgin olive oil (or meat drippings)
$^1/_4$ onion
2 TBS flour (I use fresh ground soft white wheat)
1 $^1/_2$ cups beef broth
2 tsp dried parsley
$^1/_2$ tsp onion powder
$^1/_4$ tsp garlic powder (or 2 cloves minced garlic)
$^1/_4$ tsp fresh ground black pepper
1 $^1/_2$ TBS beef soup base or bouillon (watch ingredients to avoid MSG)
1 TBS tomato ketchup

SUPPLIES:

Sharp knife/cutting board
Skillet
Whisk
Measuring cups/spoons

PREPARATION:

Thinly slice or mince onion.

DIRECTIONS:

In skillet, melt butter over medium-high heat. Add the extra virgin olive oil or meat drippings. Add the onion (and the garlic if using fresh garlic). Cook until onion is tender. Whisk in the flour. Add the broth, seasonings, soup base, and ketchup.

Bring to a boil over medium heat. Cook and stir for 2 minutes.

Reduce heat; simmer, uncovered, for 5 minutes.

 YIELD:

6 servings

 NUTRITION:

Nutrition Facts	
Serving Size 80 g	
Amount Per Serving	
Calories 80	Calories from Fat 55
	% Daily Value*
Total Fat 6.1g	9%
Saturated Fat 3.1g	15%
Trans Fat 0.0g	
Cholesterol 10mg	3%
Sodium 809mg	34%
Total Carbohydrates 4.4g	1%
Sugars 1.0g	
Protein 1.7g	
Vitamin A 4% • Vitamin C 2%	
Calcium 1% • Iron 2%	

Low in cholesterol

 NOTES:

Serve over mashed potatoes, rice, or even an open-faced roast beef sandwich (YUM).

ⓘ For Hallee the Homemaker's Wonderful Whipped Potatoes recipe, check out this link:
http://www.halleethehomemaker.com/whipped-potatoes/

ⓘ For Hallee the Homemaker's Perfect Brown Rice recipe, check out this link:
http://www.halleethehomemaker.com/brown-rice/

ⓘ For Hallee the Homemaker's Perfect White Rice recipe, check out this link:
http://www.halleethehomemaker.com/white-rice/

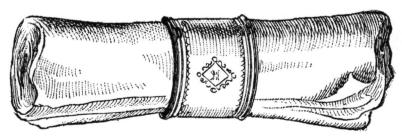

FAMILY FAVORITE STEAK & GRAVY

This is absolutely my family's favorite meal. Everyone is happy when we're having steak and gravy. It takes wonderful over mashed potatoes, and is even good over bread as leftovers.

 INGREDIENTS:

1 pound thinly sliced steak – quality doesn't matter here – you're going to cook the tenderness into it
2 TBS extra virgin olive oil
1 tsp Kosher or sea salt (Kosher or sea salt is best)
$^1/_2$ tsp fresh ground black pepper
1 white onion
1 can mushrooms
2 cups water, divided
$^1/_4$ cup flour (I use fresh ground soft white wheat)

 SUPPLIES:

Measuring cups/spoons
Sharp knife/cutting board
Deep frying pan
Whisk
Measuring cup or other container to mix flour and water for gravy

 PREPARATION:

Slice meat into strips.
Slice onion.

 DIRECTIONS:

Heat the pan over medium to medium-high heat. Add the extra virgin olive oil. Add the meat. Salt and pepper the meat. Add the onions.

Cook for about 2 minutes, then stir. Cook for about 2 more minutes, then add 1 cup water. Bring the water to a boil, then reduce the heat to low and cover.

Cook, stirring occasionally. After about 15 minutes, add the mushrooms, with the juice. Stir. Cover and continue cooking for another 20 minutes or so, stirring occasionally.

Remove the meat and veggies. Increase the heat. In a measuring cup or other container, mix $^1/_4$ cup flour with 1 cup water. When the liquid in the pan starts boiling, whisk in the water/flour mixture.

Continue whisking until the gravy boils. Boil and stir for 2 minutes.

Remove from heat. Stir the meat and veggies into the gravy.

 YIELD:

6 servings

 NUTRITION:

Nutrition Facts

Serving Size 221 g

Amount Per Serving

Calories 225	Calories from Fat 76
	% Daily Value*
Total Fat 8.5g	**13%**
Saturated Fat 2.0g	**10%**
Cholesterol 68mg	**23%**
Sodium 351mg	**15%**
Total Carbohydrates 7.1g	**2%**
Dietary Fiber 0.9g	**4%**
Sugars 1.4g	
Protein 29.2g	
Vitamin A 0%	Vitamin C 4%
Calcium 1%	Iron 17%

High in Iron

Very high in vitamin C

Low in sugar

 NOTES:

Raw beef is easier to slice when it is partially frozen.

Serve over mashed potatoes or rice.

ⓘ For Hallee the Homemaker's Wonderful Whipped Potatoes recipe, check out this link:
http://www.halleethehomemaker.com/whipped-potatoes/

ⓘ For Hallee the Homemaker's Perfect Brown Rice recipe, check out this link:
http://www.halleethehomemaker.com/brown-rice/

ⓘ For Hallee the Homemaker's Perfect White Rice recipe, check out this link:
http://www.halleethehomemaker.com/white-rice/

ROAST BEEF GRAVY

A roast beef dinner is not complete without roast beef gravy. I pour it over everything on my plate. I think the gravy is the best part of the meal.

 INGREDIENTS:

The remnants of the pan after cooking a 2-4 pound roast

$^1/_2$ cup flour (I use fresh ground soft white wheat)

Beef stock (about 1 cup – you want a total of 2 cups with the drippings in the pan)

Salt and pepper to taste (Kosher or sea salt is best/fresh ground pepper is best)

 SUPPLIES:

Whisk
Measuring cups
Lid with jar

 PREPARATION:

Prepare the roast beef. Remove it and any vegetables from the pan.

 DIRECTIONS:

If your roasting pan can be used to cook on the top of the stove, you can use it. Otherwise, you need to transfer the drippings to another pan.

Place the roasting pan on the stove and bring the juices and drippings in the pan to a boil.

Put the flour and the beef broth into a jar, cover, and shake until smooth.

Using the whisk, whisk the flour mixture into the drippings in the pan. Return to a boil. Boil and stir 2 minutes.

Salt and pepper to taste.

 YIELD:

8 servings

NUTRITION:

Nutrition Facts	
Serving Size 68 g	
Amount Per Serving	
Calories 33	Calories from Fat 2
	% Daily Value*
Total Fat 0.2g	0%
Cholesterol 0mg	0%
Sodium 196mg	8%
Total Carbohydrates 6.0g	2%
Protein 1.5g	
Vitamin A 0% •	Vitamin C 0%
Calcium 0% •	Iron 3%

Low in saturated fat

No cholesterol

Very low in sugar

High in niacin

High in selenium

High in thiamin

NOTES:

You may need to add or take out some broth, depending on how much liquid is in the drippings in the pan. You want a total of 2 cups of liquid.

COUNTRY FRIED STEAK & GRAVY

Country fried steak with creamy country gravy – this is so good. Almost "sinfully" good.

 INGREDIENTS:

For the Country Fried Steak:

2 cups flour (I use fresh-ground soft white wheat)

1 $^1/_2$ cups whole milk

2 tsp seasoned salt

$^1/_2$ tsp freshly ground black pepper

2 large eggs

$^3/_4$ tsp paprika

$^1/_4$ tsp ground red pepper

3 lbs. cube steak (tenderized round steak that's been extra tenderized)

$^1/_2$ cups extra virgin olive oil

1 TBS unsalted butter

salt (Kosher or sea salt is best)

freshly ground black pepper

For the Gravy:

$^1/_3$ cup flour (I use fresh-ground soft white wheat)

3 to 4 cups whole milk

$^1/_2$ tsp seasoned salt

freshly ground black pepper

 SUPPLIES:

2 shallow dishes for coating the steaks

Deep skillet

Tongs

Paper-towel lined plate

Measuring cups/spoons

Whisk

 PREPARATION:

Mix the eggs and the milk in a shallow dish.

Mix the flour, seasoned salt, black pepper, paprika, and red pepper together in a shallow dish.

 DIRECTIONS:

Sprinkle each steak with salt and fresh ground black pepper. Dip each steak into the egg/milk mixture, then coat it on both sides with the flour mixture. Repeat for all steaks.

Heat oil in large skillet over medium heat. Add the butter.

Cook the meat, 3 pieces at a time, until the edges start to look golden brown – about 2 minutes each side. Using tongs, remove the meat to a paper towel-lined plate. Repeat until all the meat is cooked.

Discard all of the grease in the pan but $\frac{1}{4}$ cup of it. Heat it back up over medium-high heat. Sprinkle the flour evenly over the grease. Using a whisk, mix the flour with the grease, creating a golden-brown paste. Add more flour if it looks overly greasy; add a little more grease if it becomes too pasty/clumpy. Keep cooking until the roux reaches a deep golden brown color.

Pour in the milk, whisking constantly. Taste and add seasoned salt and/or black pepper to taste. Cook, whisking, until the gravy is smooth and thick, 5 to 10 minutes. Be prepared to add more milk if it becomes overly thick.

 YIELD:

6 servings

 NUTRITION:

Nutrition Facts

Serving Size 498 g

Amount Per Serving	
Calories 924	Calories from Fat 344
	% Daily Value*
Total Fat 38.2g	59%
Saturated Fat 11.5g	58%
Cholesterol 290mg	97%
Sodium 847mg	35%
Total Carbohydrates 45.8g	15%
Dietary Fiber 1.5g	6%
Sugars 9.9g	
Protein 95.0g	
Vitamin A 10% •	Vitamin C 0%
Calcium 23% •	Iron 57%

High in selenium

High in vitamin B12

 NOTES:

Serve with mashed potatoes.

ⓘ For Hallee the Homemaker's Wonderful Whipped Potatoes recipe, check out this link:

http://www.halleethehomemaker.com/whipped-potatoes/

CATCH UP TO TOMATO GRAVY

Today, tomatoes are very popular for sauce and gravy making. Neither a fruit nor a vegetable, tomatoes are technically a berry. They have a versatile flavor and texture that works with all kinds of meats or simply pasta. They have a high liquid content and soft flesh that breaks down so that other thickening agents need not be added. They are also incredibly good for you, packed with vitamins, minerals, and flavenoids like the anti-oxidant lycopene. Tomatoes are a great source of Vitamin E (Alpha Tocopherol), Thiamin, Niacin, Vitamin B6, Folate, Vitamin A, Vitamin C, Vitamin K, Magnesium, Phosphorus, Copper, Calcium, Iron, Potassium, Manganese, and are a very good source of Dietary Fiber.

Using tomato as a base for gravy is a relatively new idea to the culinary world. The first time it is recorded as being used for the base of a gravy is in 1905 in *The Times Cookbook*, for a recipe for "Beef, Tomato Gravy," which is identified as a Spanish Recipe.

In 1955, tomato gravy was introduced in an advertisement with meat loaf: "…it is truly delicious with this savoury tomato gravy!"

This section contains "tomato gravies" covering anything from a traditional Ghanian dish to gravy intended to be served with southern style Buttermilk Biscuits. All of them have delicious, nutritious tomatoes as their base. Some are vegetarian, and some contain meat.

GRATIFYING GHANAIAN TRAMMELED TOMATO GRAVY

GHANAIAN TOMATO GRAVY

This is a popular dish from the country of Ghana. It is so quick and easy to make, and the simple ingredients are full of flavor. The thyme and cayenne pepper give the sauce a bit of a kick. It is perfect served over rice, and makes a wonderful meatless meal.

INGREDIENTS:

2 medium onions

1 green pepper

8 Roma tomatoes

$^{1}/_{2}$ cup extra virgin olive oil

1 tsp cayenne pepper

1 tsp seasoned salt

1 tsp fresh thyme

SUPPLIES:

Sharp knife/cutting board

Deep skillet

Measuring cups/spoons

PREPARATION:

Dice onion and green pepper ⓘ

Dice tomatoes

DIRECTIONS:

Heat oil over medium-high heat. Add onion. Sauté until soft.

Add green peppers, tomatoes, and seasoning.

Heat, stirring regularly, about 30 minutes.

YIELD:

6 servings

NUTRITION:

Nutrition Facts	
Serving Size 240 g	
Amount Per Serving	
Calories 194	Calories from Fat 155
	% Daily Value*
Total Fat 17.3g	27%
Saturated Fat 2.5g	12%
Cholesterol 0mg	0%
Sodium 264mg	11%
Total Carbohydrates 11.0g	4%
Dietary Fiber 3.1g	12%
Sugars 6.4g	
Protein 2.1g	
Vitamin A 31% • Vitamin C 66%	
Calcium 3% • Iron 5%	

No cholesterol

High in vitamin A

Very high in vitamin C

NOTES:

Serve over rice.

ⓘ For Hallee the Homemaker's Perfect Brown Rice recipe, check out this link: http://www.halleethehomemaker.com/brown-rice/

ⓘ For Hallee the Homemaker's Perfect White Rice recipe, check out this link: http://www.halleethehomemaker.com/white-rice/

ⓘ For information about a tip for chopping onions, follow this link: http://www.halleethehomemaker.com/chopping-veg/

IMPRISONED ITALIAN TOMATO GRAVY

ITALIAN TOMATO GRAVY

Yes – I know this is spaghetti sauce. But, it's a sauce served over noodles. We'll consider it a shade of gravy for this recipe book.

INGREDIENTS:

2 cans (or 1 large can) organic stewed tomatoes, with the juice and
3 small cans organic tomato sauce
– OR –
about a 16 oz (4-6) garden fresh tomatoes, stewed
about 1 lbs Turkey sausage
2 Tbs extra virgin olive oil
1 medium onion, chopped ①
3 cloves garlic, finely diced
$^{1}/_{2}$ tablespoon salt, Kosher or sea salt is best
1 teaspoon black pepper
2 tablespoons brown sugar or honey
1 tablespoon dried oregano
1 tablespoon dried parsley
2 teaspoons dried basil
1 teaspoon dried sage
1 bay leaf
1 small can organic tomato paste

SUPPLIES:
skillet
pasta pan
sauce pan
spoons/ladles
clean cutting board for meat
good sharp knife
cheese grater (if serving with fresh ground parmesan)

PREPARATION:
Prior to beginning, you may want to measure and combine all of your dry spices and seasonings into a single bowl or ramekin so you can easily add them into the sauce all at once.
Sauce will take a minimum of 1 hour to simmer. After an hour, you may want to have some bread handy for dipping and taste testing.

DIRECTIONS:

Remove sausage from skin and cook over medium heat in the bottom of a large pot. This is not a fatty meat, so you'll need to add about 2 TBS extra virgin olive oil to the bottom of the pan. When it's brown, add one onion, chopped. Cook until tender.

Add 3 cloves garlic, finely diced. Cook about 5 minutes longer.

Add 2 cans (or 1 large can) stewed tomatoes, with the juice (break the tomatoes up or chop them up).

Add 3 small cans tomato sauce and 1 small can tomato paste. Stir in $^1/_2$ tablespoon salt, 1 teaspoon black pepper, 2 tablespoons brown sugar or honey, 1 tablespoon dried oregano, 1 tablespoon dried parsley, 2 teaspoons dried basil, 1 teaspoon dried sage, 1 bay leaf.

Bring to a boil, then reduce heat to low, cover, and simmer for at least 1 hour, stirring regularly. The longer it simmers, the more the spices have a chance to infuse the sauce. After about an hour, taste it and see if it needs more sugar, or more salt, or a touch more oregano. Let your tongue guide you. Add a little bit at a time, give it a few minutes to blend in with the flavors, then taste it again. (A good way to taste is to dip a bit of bread in it.)

YIELD:

About 2 quarts of sauce / about 8 healthy servings.

NUTRITION:

Nutrition Facts	
Serving Size 215 g	

Amount Per Serving	
Calories 296	Calories from Fat 179
	% Daily Value
Total Fat 19.9g	**31%**
Saturated Fat 5.7g	**29%**
Trans Fat 0.1g	
Cholesterol 48mg	**16%**
Sodium 823mg	**34%**
Total Carbohydrates 17.1g	**6%**
Dietary Fiber 3.5g	**14%**
Sugars 11.4g	
Protein 14.0g	
Vitamin A 31% • Vitamin C 40%	
Calcium 5% • Iron 15%	

High in vitamin A

High in vitamin C

NOTES:

If you are avoiding pork, make sure that the sausage casings are also pork free. They are often made with pork products. The safest way is to just buy Kosher in this case.

Whole grain pastas are not all alike. Be sure to be choosy, or make your own.

ⓘ For information about a tip for chopping onions, follow this link: http://www.halleethehomemaker.com/chopping-veg/

VEGETARIAN TOMATO GRAVY

This is an incredibly southern dish – as in a south Georgia/Alabama/Mississippi or northern Florida kind of tradition. Tomato gravy is traditionally made with sausage drippings. Since we don't eat pork, here is a variation that ends up tasting perfectly delicious. Serve it over grits (YUM), biscuits ①, or simply over toast.

INGREDIENTS:

$^1/_4$ cup unsalted butter
1 medium onion
3 green onions
1 stalk celery
$^1/_4$ cup green pepper
4 oz can mushrooms, drained
2 TBS flour (I use fresh ground, soft white wheat)
Enough vegetable broth to add to tomato juices to make 1 cup
14 $^1/_2$ oz can diced tomatoes
Salt and pepper to taste (Kosher or sea salt is best/fresh ground pepper is best)

SUPPLIES:

Sharp knife/cutting board
Skillet
Measuring cups/spoons
Whisk

PREPARATION:

Drain the tomatoes into a measuring cup. Add enough chicken broth to make 1 cup.
Finely chop the green onions.
Dice the onion. ①
Dice the celery.
Dice the green pepper.
Dice the mushrooms.

DIRECTIONS:

Melt the butter in the skillet over medium-high heat. Add the onions, celery, green pepper, and mushrooms. Cook until onions are tender. Stir in the flour.

Whisk until smooth.

Whisk in the tomato juice/vegetable broth. Continue stirring until mixture thickens and boils. Stir in tomatoes.

Continue to stir until tomatoes are heated through.

YIELD:

4 servings

NUTRITION:

Nutrition Facts

Serving Size 172 g

Amount Per Serving	
Calories 114	Calories from Fat 72
	% Daily Value*
Total Fat 8.0g	12%
Saturated Fat 4.9g	25%
Cholesterol 20mg	7%
Sodium 412mg	17%
Total Carbohydrates 9.1g	3%
Dietary Fiber 2.3g	9%
Sugars 3.9g	
Protein 2.5g	
Vitamin A 13% •	Vitamin C 19%
Calcium 3% •	Iron 4%

High in vitamin A
High in vitamin C

NOTES:

Serve over grits or biscuits.

ⓘ For Hallee the Homemaker's Whole Wheat Buttermilk Biscuits, check out this link:
http://www.halleethehomemaker.com/buttermilk-biscuits/

ⓘ For information about a tip for chopping onions, follow this link:
http://www.halleethehomemaker.com/chopping-veg/

TOMATO GRAVY

The beef bacon and the onion with the tomato – oh yum. Serve it over biscuits ⓘ and watch your family inhale it.

INGREDIENTS:

$^1/_2$ pound sliced beef bacon
1 small onion
2 TBS flour (I use fresh ground soft white wheat)
1/8 tsp salt (Kosher or sea salt is best)
Pinch fresh ground pepper
14 $^1/_2$ ounces diced tomatoes, undrained
3 cups tomato juice

SUPPLIES:

Sharp knife/cutting board
Skillet
Plate lined with paper towels
Measuring cups/spoons
Wooden spoon/whisk

PREPARATION:

Dice the bacon.
Chop the onion. ⓘ

DIRECTIONS:

In a skillet, cook bacon over medium-high heat until crisp. Remove from pan and drain on plate lined with paper towels. Discard all but 2 TBS of the grease and drippings.

Cook onion in the drippings until tender. Whisk in the flour, salt and pepper.

Cook and stir over low heat until mixture is golden brown.

Gradually add tomatoes and tomato juice; stir well.

Bring to a boil over medium heat. Cook and stir for 2 minutes.

Reduce heat; simmer, uncovered, for 10-15 minutes or until thickened, stirring occasionally. Stir in bacon.

YIELD:

8 servings

NUTRITION:

Nutrition Facts

Serving Size 360 g

Amount Per Serving

Calories 186	Calories from Fat 31
	% Daily Value*
Total Fat 3.4g	5%
Saturated Fat 0.6g	3%
Cholesterol 51mg	17%
Sodium 797mg	33%
Total Carbohydrates 16.2g	5%
Dietary Fiber 2.3g	9%
Sugars 9.8g	
Protein 12.0g	

Vitamin A 33%	•	Vitamin C 79%
Calcium 3%	•	Iron 11%

Low in saturated fat

High in potassium

High in vitamin A

Very high in vitamin C

NOTES:

Serve over grits or biscuits.

ⓘ For Hallee the Homemaker's Whole Wheat Buttermilk Biscuits, check out this link:
http://www.halleethehomemaker.com/buttermilk-biscuits/

ⓘ For information about a tip for chopping onions, follow this link:
http://www.halleethehomemaker.com/chopping-veg/

SAUCY MEATBALLS

Meatballs have been around for thousands of years and in almost every meat-eating culture. One of the earliest references to a meatball in a recipe book can be found in a Roman cookbook dated in the first century A.D called *"De re coquinaria libri decem (Cuisine in Ten Books)"*

Meatballs are SO versatile. You can use different kinds of ground meats - turkey, beef, lamb, fish, etc. - and any number of flavorings to create the meatball. Add to that the wonderful array of choices of sauces and gravies to pair with the meatball, and you could potentially have a different meal every night for weeks.

Most of the meatballs in this section are made with ground beef. You can almost always substitute meats like ground turkey or ground bison or even ground lamb for ground beef and still maintain the integrity of the dish. Just remember that turkey and bison have a lower fat content than beef, while lamb has a slightly higher fat content, so your recipes will need adjustment to accommodate the differences.

Meatball dishes are wonderful to serve when you have company coming. You can easily adjust recipes to feed larger crowds, and everyone enjoys a good meatball. Serve these gravy dishes over rice, pastas, or mashed potatoes – or stick some toothpicks in the meatballs in their gravy bath and serve them as appetizers at a party.

BRAISED MEATBALLS IN RED-WINE GRAVY

This is a simple yet flavorful dish. It is a perfect company-coming meal. Serve with saffron rice or homemade noodles.

INGREDIENTS:
1 6-ounce piece day-old French bread ⓘ with crust
1 cup whole milk
1 $^3/_4$ lbs. grass fed ground beef
2 large eggs
1 medium onion
$^1/_2$ cup plus 1 TBS fresh Italian parsley
2 tsp salt (Kosher or sea salt is best)
1 tsp fresh ground black pepper
1 tsp dried summer savory ⓘ
Flour for dredging meatballs
2 TBS unsalted butter
1 $^1/_2$ tsp extra virgin olive oil
2 cups dry red wine ⓘ
$^1/_4$ cup tomato paste
Salt and pepper to taste (Kosher or sea salt is best/fresh ground pepper is best)
3 cups canned beef broth (watch for MSG in ingredients)

SUPPLIES:
Food processor.
Mixing bowl for meatballs
Two 13x9 glass baking dishes
Large skillet
Sharp knife/cutting board
Small bowls
Whisk
Wooden spoon
Measuring cups/spoons

PREPARATION:
Preheat oven to 350° F (175° C).
Cut bread into 8 pieces. In a small bowl, submerge bread in milk and let stand for 10 minutes.
Finely chop onion ⓘ.
Chop the parsley.

DIRECTIONS:

Squeeze most of the milk out of the bread. Discard the leftover milk. Place the bread in large bowl. Add ground beef, eggs, onion, $^1/_2$ cup of the parsley, salt, pepper, and dried summer savory. Mix well.

Add mixture to food processor. Mix until blended and looks pasty.

Form into 1 $^3/_4$ inches meatballs (will make about 30). Place in 13x9 baking dishes. Bake for 30 minutes.

Remove from oven and let slightly cool.

Dust meatballs with flour.

Melt butter with the oil in the skillet over medium-high heat. Working in batches, brown the meatballs on all sides – about 3 minutes. When all meatballs are browned, return them all to the pan.

Whisk wine and tomato paste in a small bowl. Add to the meatballs. Increase heat and bring to a boil.

Boil, stirring frequently, for 5 minutes. Add beef broth, reduce heat to medium, and simmer until flavors blend and gravy thickens, stirring frequently, about 15 minutes.

Season with salt and pepper to taste.

Sprinkle with remaining parsley.

YIELD:

6 servings

NUTRITION:

Nutrition Facts	
Serving Size 101 g	
Amount Per Serving	
Calories 103	Calories from Fat 45
	% Daily Value*
Total Fat 5.0g	8%
Saturated Fat 2.2g	11%
Cholesterol 38mg	13%
Sodium 314mg	13%
Total Carbohydrates 2.8g	1%
Sugars 1.3g	
Protein 7.9g	
Vitamin A 4% • Vitamin C 5%	
Calcium 3% • Iron 7%	

High in Vitamin A

High in Vitamin C

High in Iron

NOTES:

ⓘ You can substitute thyme for the summer savory.

ⓘ Here is Hallee the Homemaker's Whole Wheat French Bread Recipe: http://www.halleethehomemaker.com/2009/08/french-bread/

ⓘ For information about a tip for chopping onions, follow this link: http://www.halleethehomemaker.com/chopping-veg/

ⓘ If you abstain from alcohol even in cooking, in that case you can substitute a 100% pure white or dark grape juice (make sure there is no apple juice in it) along with one teaspoon of distilled vinegar to approximate the same flavor and properties while cooking.

SWEDISH MEATBALLS & GRAVY

My children love this dish. Meatballs are always fun, and the simple beef flavors make this a very "comfort food" style entrée.

INGREDIENTS:

1 lb. grass fed ground beef
6 ounces French bread ⓘ
$^1/_4$ cup whole milk
1 small onion
1 egg
1 TBS fresh parsley
$^1/_4$ tsp ground cloves
$^1/_4$ tsp ground allspice
4 TBS unsalted butter
2 TBS flour (I use fresh ground soft white wheat)
1 $^1/_2$ cup beef broth
$^1/_2$ tsp soy sauce
1 tsp Worcestershire sauce
Salt and pepper to taste (Kosher or sea salt is best/fresh ground pepper is best)

SUPPLIES:

Large bowl
Deep skillet
Slotted spoon
Cheese grater
Whisk

PREPARATION:

Grate onion
Chop parsley

DIRECTIONS:

Soak bread in milk. Using your fingers, break the submerged bread apart until the milk has the consistency of a thick batter. Add the meat, onion, egg, parsley, cloves, and allspice, mixing thoroughly. Shape into small balls.

Melt butter in skillet over medium-high heat. Brown meatballs on all sides. Remove from the skillet with a slotted spoon.

Whisk flour into the skillet, mixing with the butter. Whisk in the beef broth. Stir until smooth. Add soy sauce and Worcestershire sauce. Add salt and pepper to taste.

Place the meatballs in the gravy. Reduce heat to medium-low. Cover and cook for 10 minutes.

YIELD:

4 servings

NUTRITION:

Nutrition Facts

Serving Size 311 g

Amount Per Serving

Calories 489	Calories from Fat 230
	% Daily Value*
Total Fat 25.5g	39%
Saturated Fat 12.8g	64%
Trans Fat 0.0g	
Cholesterol 148mg	49%
Sodium 794mg	33%
Total Carbohydrates 30.3g	10%
Dietary Fiber 1.5g	6%
Sugars 3.3g	
Protein 32.6g	

Vitamin A 10%	•	Vitamin C 5%
Calcium 8%	•	Iron 28%

Low in sugar

High in iron

NOTES:

Serve over rice or noodles.

ⓘ Find Hallee the Homemaker's Whole Wheat French Bread Recipe here: http://www.halleethehomemaker.com/2009/08/french-bread/

ⓘ For Hallee the Homemaker's Perfect Brown Rice recipe, check out this link: http://www.halleethehomemaker.com/brown-rice/

ⓘ For Hallee the Homemaker's Perfect White Rice recipe, check out this link: http://www.halleethehomemaker.com/white-rice/

BITE-SIZED BAKED MEATBALLS IN MALLEABLE MUSHROOM GRAVY

BAKED MEATBALLS IN MUSHROOM GRAVY

The meatballs cook in the oven in the gravy in this dish to make a delicious, comfort-food meat. This would be perfect to take to a church potlock or to have ready to come out of the oven on a busy night. Throw together a quick salad and serve over rice with some French Bread and you have a winning meal.

INGREDIENTS:

1 lb ground grass fed ground beef
1 medium onion
1 cup uncooked white rice
1 egg
1 tsp salt (Kosher or sea salt is best)
1 tsp fresh ground black pepper
1 cup bread crumbs
1 cup whole milk
1 recipe of "No-Cans" Can-Do Cream of Mushroom Soup ⓘ
$^{3}/_{4}$ tsp Worcestershire sauce

SUPPLIES:

Large bowl
Measuring cups/spoons
Baking sheet
Skillet

PREPARATION:

Prepare "cream of mushroom soup"
Finely mince onion.
Beat egg
Heat milk to hot (but not boiling)
Preheat oven to 400° F (200° C)

DIRECTIONS:

Mix beef, onion, rice, egg, salt, pepper, bread crumbs, and hot milk together. Mix thoroughly. Shape into golf ball sized balls. Place in baking dish.

Whisk together soup, milk, and Worcestershire sauce.

Pour over meatballs.

Cover tightly and bake at 400° F for 30 minutes.

YIELD:

4 servings

NUTRITION:

Nutrition Facts

Serving Size 436 g

Amount Per Serving	
Calories 597	Calories from Fat 175
	% Daily Value*
Total Fat 19.4g	30%
Saturated Fat 7.0g	35%
Cholesterol 121mg	40%
Sodium 1370mg	57%
Total Carbohydrates 67.1g	22%
Dietary Fiber 2.4g	10%
Sugars 7.1g	
Protein 34.9g	
Vitamin A 2% • Vitamin C 4%	
Calcium 11% • Iron 40%	

High in vitamin B6

High in vitamin B12

NOTES:

Serve over rice ⓘ or noodles.

I do not use canned soups, so I make my own cream of mushroom soup.
ⓘ Find Hallee the Homemaker's "No-Cans" Can-Do Cream of Mushroom Soup Recipe here:
http://www.halleethehomemaker.com/cream-of-mushroom/

ⓘ For Hallee the Homemaker's Perfect Brown Rice recipe, check out this link:
http://www.halleethehomemaker.com/brown-rice/

ⓘ For Hallee the Homemaker's Perfect White Rice recipe, check out this link:
http://www.halleethehomemaker.com/white-rice/

MOUTHWATERING MUSHROOMS & GRAVY

Mushrooms and gravy just seem to go hand-in-hand. Mixed with broth or wine, some butter or onion, they make the absolute perfect flavor combination to go with just about any kind of meal.

Mushroom gravies have been around for as long as there have been cookbooks. Ancient Romans even used to barter with the valuable truffles that are such a delicacy even in our day.

Store them in the refrigerator, but don't wash them. Just use a damp cloth to wipe them clean before cooking with them.

My favorite recipe in this book is the Wild Mushroom & Shallot Gravy. The roasted onion and garlic combined with the wild mushroom mix makes an amazing gourmet-style sauce right in my very kitchen.

MALLEABLE MUSHROOM GRAVY

MUSHROOM GRAVY

This is a handy recipe to have for meat loaf, or roast beef, or simply grilled steak. It's easy, it's delicious, and it's satisfying.

 INGREDIENTS:

3 fresh mushrooms

2 green onions

1 TBS unsalted butter

1 TBS flour (I use fresh ground soft white wheat)

1 cup beef broth

Salt and pepper to taste (Kosher or sea salt is best/fresh ground pepper is best)

 SUPPLIES:

Sharp knife and cutting board.

Skillet

Wooden spoon

Whisk

 PREPARATION:

Dice mushrooms

Chop onions ①

 DIRECTIONS:

Sauté mushrooms and onions in butter for 5 minutes over medium heat. Whisk in flour until smooth. Whisk in beef broth.

Heat to boiling. Reduce heat and simmer for 5 minutes.

 YIELD:

4 servings

NUTRITION:

Nutrition Facts	
Serving Size 77 g	
Amount Per Serving	
Calories 45	Calories from Fat 29
	% Daily Value*
Total Fat 3.3g	5%
Saturated Fat 1.9g	10%
Cholesterol 8mg	3%
Sodium 213mg	9%
Total Carbohydrates 2.4g	1%
Protein 1.7g	
Vitamin A 3% •	Vitamin C 3%
Calcium 1% •	Iron 3%

High in niacin
Very high in vitamin B6

NOTES:

You can substitute 2 TBS of the broth for 2 TBS dry red wine for an extra kick of flavor.

ⓘ For information about a tip for chopping onions, follow this link: http://www.halleethehomemaker.com/chopping-veg/

WELTED WILD MUSHROOM SHACKLED SHALLOT GRAVY

WILD MUSHROOM-SHALLOT GRAVY

This gravy is so amazing served over chicken. Don't substitute the Marsala for another kind of wine, though. You want the sweetness of this wine in this sauce. Whole Foods and Trader Joes have beautiful pre-mixed wild mushroom packs from which you can choose for this recipe.

INGREDIENTS:

$^1/_4$ cup extra virgin olive oil
10 shallots
4 garlic cloves
12 ounces mixed wild mushrooms (oyster, morel, stemmed shiitake, etc.)
1 TBS fresh rosemary
1 TBS fresh thyme
2 tsp fresh sage
$^1/_2$ cup Marsala wine ⓘ
$^1/_2$ cup dry Sherry ⓘ
1 $^1/_2$ cups chicken stock
1 cup heavy whipping cream

SUPPLIES:

Sharp knife/cutting board
Measuring cups/spoons
Heavy skillet
Small glass baking dish
Foil

PREPARATION:

Preheat oven to 300° F (150° C)
Slice the mushrooms.
Peel the shallots.
Peel the garlic.
Chop fresh herbs.

DIRECTIONS:

Combine oil, shallots, and garlic in small glass baking dish. Cover tightly with foil. Bake 1 hour. Cool until you can handle the shallots and garlic, then thinly slice. Reserve the oil.

Put 1 TBS of the oil from the dish into the skillet. Heat over medium-high heat. Add mushrooms, rosemary, thyme, sage, roasted, shallots, and garlic. Sauté until mushrooms are tender – about 5 minutes.

Add the wines. Boil until syrupy – about 6 minutes.

Add the chicken stock. Boil until it is reduced by half – about 10 minutes.

Add cream. Boil until it thickens – about 5 minutes.

Season to taste with salt and pepper.

 YIELD:

3 cups (6 servings)

 NUTRITION:

Nutrition Facts		
Serving Size 204 g		
Amount Per Serving		
Calories 212		Calories from Fat 146
		% Daily Value*
Total Fat 16.3g		25%
Saturated Fat 5.9g		30%
Cholesterol 27mg		9%
Sodium 205mg		9%
Total Carbohydrates 7.5g		3%
Dietary Fiber 1.1g		4%
Sugars 1.3g		
Protein 3.0g		
Vitamin A 11%	•	Vitamin C 7%
Calcium 5%	•	Iron 15%

Low in sugar

Very high in vitamin B6

 NOTES:

Best served with chicken or turkey or other game fowl.

The onions and garlic can be roasted the day before.

ⓘ If you abstain from alcohol even in cooking, in that case you can substitute a 100% pure white or dark grape juice (make sure there is no apple juice in it) along with one teaspoon of distilled vinegar to approximate the same flavor and properties while cooking.

CONFINED IN A CROCK POT ROAST WITH MANACLED
MUSHROOM GRAVY

CROCK POT ROAST IN MUSHROOM GRAVY

Your whole house will smell absolutely amazing in the 6-hours it takes for this roast to cook in the crock pot. Once you try it, this recipe will be a staple in your home.

INGREDIENTS:

2-pound chuck roast

1 cup sour cream

1 cup fresh mushrooms

1 envelope dry onion soup mix (watch for MSG in ingredients)

1 cup water

1 recipe of "No-Cans" Can-Do Cream of Mushroom Soup ⓘ

SUPPLIES:

Crock pot
Wooden spoon

PREPARATION:

Slice mushrooms.
Prepare cream of mushroom soup.

DIRECTIONS:

Place the roast in the crock pot. Mix all of the remaining ingredients together and pour over the roast. Cook on low heat for 6 hours.

YIELD:

6 servings

NUTRITION:

Nutrition Facts		
Serving Size 346 g		
Amount Per Serving		
Calories 472	Calories from Fat 211	
	% Daily Value*	
Total Fat 23.5g		36%
Saturated Fat 10.2g		51%
Cholesterol 170mg		57%
Sodium 958mg		40%
Total Carbohydrates 9.5g		3%
Dietary Fiber 0.6g		2%
Sugars 1.3g		
Protein 52.8g		
Vitamin A 5%	•	Vitamin C 1%
Calcium 8%	•	Iron 37%

Very low in sugar

High in selenium

High in vitamin B6

High in vitamin B12

High in zinc

NOTES:

You can cook it on high for 3 hours, but it is better if cooked on low heat. The meat will be more tender.

I do not use canned cream of mushroom soup.

ⓘ Find Hallee the Homemaker's "No-Cans" Can-Do Cream of Mushroom Soup Recipe here:
http://www.halleethehomemaker.com/cream-of-mushroom/

HEMMED IN HAMBURGER PATTY CASSEROLE WITH MEEK MUSHROOM GRAVY

HAMBURGER PATTY CASSEROLE WITH MUSHROOM GRAVY

This is one of those "perfect comfort food" meals. Stick it in the oven and 45-minutes later you have a meat and potatoes dish swimming in mushroom gravy.

INGREDIENTS:

1 $^1/_2$ lbs grass-fed ground beef
$^1/_4$ cup extra virgin olive oil
$^1/_4$ cup flour (I use fresh ground soft white wheat)
2 cups beef broth
6 oz. fresh mushrooms
4 medium potatoes
$^1/_2$ tsp fresh ground pepper
$^1/_2$ tsp salt (Kosher or sea salt is best)

SUPPLIES:

Skillet
Sharp knife/cutting board
2-quart casserole dish with lid

PREPARATION:

Slice the mushrooms.
Scrub the potatoes and thinly slice.
Form the beef into 6 each $^1/_4$ lb. Patties.
Preheat oven to 400° F (200° C)

DIRECTIONS:

Heat the skillet to medium-high heat. Sprinkle the beef patties with $^1/_2$ tsp salt and the pepper. Cook them until brown on both sides. Remove from pan.

Add the olive oil to the pan. Whisk in the flour until smooth. Whisk in the beef broth. Bring to a boil, whisking regularly. Boil for 1-2 minutes. Stir in the mushrooms.

Line the bottom of the casserole with the patties of meat. Top with the sliced potatoes. Sprinkle with the remaining salt. Pour the gravy over the top.

Cover tightly and bake at 400° F (200° C) for 45 minutes, or until the potatoes are cooked through.

YIELD:

6 servings

NUTRITION:

Nutrition Facts

Serving Size 379 g

Amount Per Serving

Calories 409	Calories from Fat 182
	% Daily Value*
Total Fat 20.2g	31%
Saturated Fat 5.9g	30%
Cholesterol 75mg	25%
Sodium 728mg	30%
Total Carbohydrates 27.6g	9%
Dietary Fiber 3.9g	16%
Sugars 2.4g	
Protein 28.5g	

Vitamin A 0%	•	Vitamin C 48%
Calcium 4%	•	Iron 26%

Low in sugar

Very high in vitamin B6

High in vitamin C

NOTES:

If you desired, you could throw in some frozen mixed vegetables as part of the layering process between the potatoes and the gravy. That makes a full meal in one pan and tastes amazing.

GOBBLER GRAVY

I believe that the gravy is one of the most important elements in a holiday meal. Dry turkey, plain mashed potatoes, an uninteresting plate – a savory, flavorful homemade gravy can redeem any of it. Once you learn how truly easy it is to make your own gravy, and how amazing you can make it taste, you'll never crack open another gravy jar (eww, by the way) again.

There are so many different ways to make turkey gravy – with white wine, with apple cider, with giblets and egg, or even a simple broth-style gravy. Play around with different spices and see what you and your family like best.

TURKEY CIDER GRAVY

The apple cider in this recipe gives this gravy a nice kick. You will love the clean apple flavors with the turkey. This could easily become your family's favorite turkey gravy.

INGREDIENTS:

12-pound turkey including neck and giblets (excluding liver)
3 stalks celery
3 carrots
2 medium onions
1 bay leaf
4 sprigs parsley
10 cups pure filtered water
12-ounce bottle of apple cider
$^1/_2$ cup flour (I use fresh ground soft white wheat)

SUPPLIES:

Roasting pan for turkey
Large saucepan
Sharp knife/cutting board
Strainer
Whisk
Wooden spoon
Measuring cups

PREPARATION:

I have directions on my Hallee the Homemaker website to help you Roast the Perfect Turkey ⓘ.
Chop celery into 2-inch pieces.
Chop carrots into 2-inch pieces.
Chop the onions into quarters.

DIRECTIONS:

While the turkey is roasting, in a large saucepan place the neck, giblets, celery, onions, bay leaf, parsley, and 10 cups of water. Bring to a boil.

Reduce heat to low. Skim the foam off of the top of the water and let simmer for 1 hour.

Strain the broth and discard the solids. If the remaining liquid is less than 6 cups, add enough filtered water to equal six cups.

When the turkey is finished roasting, transfer the turkey to a serving platter. Place the roasting pan on the stove across two burners. If your pan cannot be put on the stovetop (disposable aluminum pans cannot be placed on stovetop), then transfer the drippings and browned bits to a saucepan.) Cook the drippings over medium-high heat, scraping the bottom with a wooden spoon, until it comes to a boil. Cook until syrupy. Add the cider and continue to boil for 6 to 10 minutes – until a syrup forms.

Whisk in the flour and cook, stirring constantly, 2 minutes.

Gradually stir in the giblet broth. Bring to a simmer and cook, stirring often, 15 to 20 minutes.

Season to taste with Kosher salt and fresh ground black pepper.

 YIELD:

4 cups (8 servings)

 NUTRITION:

Nutrition Facts

Serving Size 417 g

Amount Per Serving	
Calories 178	Calories from Fat 115
	% Daily Value*
Total Fat 12.8g	20%
Saturated Fat 1.8g	9%
Trans Fat 0.0g	
Cholesterol 0mg	0%
Sodium 33mg	1%
Total Carbohydrates 16.0g	5%
Dietary Fiber 1.5g	6%
Sugars 7.0g	
Protein 1.4g	
Vitamin A 78% •	Vitamin C 8%
Calcium 3% •	Iron 4%

High in vitamin A

Low sodium

 NOTES:

If you want a smoother gravy, you can strain the result through a fine-mesh sieve.

Keep warm until time to serve.

ⓘ You can find Hallee the Homemaker's instructions on how to roast the perfect turkey here:
http://www.halleethehomemaker.com/perfect-bird/

SUBMISSIVE TRUSSED TURKEY SAWMILL GRAVY

TURKEY SAWMILL GRAVY

Biscuits and gravy are a favorite in my part of the world (Kentucky). I do things a little different in my house, though – whole wheat biscuits ① and turkey sausage gravy. This is my 4-year-old's favorite breakfast, and all of the family is excited when they see it on the menu.

INGREDIENTS:

1 lb. turkey breakfast sausage
$^1/_4$ cup extra virgin olive oil
$^1/_4$ cup flour (I use fresh ground soft white wheat)
2 cups milk
$^1/_2$ tsp salt (Kosher or sea salt is best)
$^1/_2$ tsp fresh ground pepper

SUPPLIES:

skillet
Measuring cups/spoons
Wooden spoon
Slotted spoon and dish for holding cooked sausage
Whisk

PREPARATION:

Crumble the sausage into the skillet and cook over medium-high heat until browned thoroughly. Using a slotted spoon, remove the sausage from the pan and set it aside.

DIRECTIONS:

Add the extra virgin olive oil to the pan. Whisk it in and pick up the browned pieces of sausage on the bottom of the pan. Whisk in the flour. Stir until a smooth paste forms.

Slowly whisk in the milk. Stir until it comes to a boil. Continue boiling and stirring for 2 minutes. Remove from heat. Stir in the salt, pepper, and cooked sausage.

YIELD:

8 servings

NUTRITION:

Nutrition Facts

Serving Size 129 g

Amount Per Serving	
Calories 221	Calories from Fat 159
	% Daily Value*
Total Fat 17.7g	27%
Saturated Fat 1.7g	8%
Cholesterol 51mg	17%
Sodium 577mg	24%
Total Carbohydrates 5.9g	2%
Sugars 3.1g	
Protein 11.5g	
Vitamin A 0% •	Vitamin C 0%
Calcium 1% •	Iron 11%

Very high in vitamin B6

Very high in vitamin B12

NOTES:

Serve over biscuits or fried potatoes.

ⓘ For Hallee the Homemaker's Whole Wheat Buttermilk Biscuits, check out this link:http://www.halleethehomemaker.com/buttermilk-biscuits/

ⓘ For Hallee the Homemaker's Family Fit Fried Potatoes recipe, check out this link:
http://www.halleethehomemaker.com/skillet-taters/

TURKEY HAM GRAVY

Turkey ham is always nice for a quick meal. Fry it up, make a quick gravy in the skillet, and serve with fried potatoes or rice. It's great as a different meat in the mornings or for brunch, too. The gravy is peppery and wonderful with the smoky meat.

INGREDIENTS:

4 Turkey ham steaks
4 TBS unsalted butter
3 TBS flour (I use fresh ground soft white wheat)
1 $^1/_4$ cup whole milk
$^1/_2$ tsp salt (Kosher or sea salt is best)
$^1/_4$ tsp fresh ground black pepper
$^1/_4$ tsp onion powder

SUPPLIES:

Skillet
Measuring cups/spoons
Whisk

PREPARATION:

Fry the turkey ham steaks in 2 TBS butter over medium high heat until heated through and browned to preference. Remove from the pan.

DIRECTIONS:

In the pan you cooked the turkey ham steaks, melt the remaining 2 TBS butter, scraping up and blending in any of the browned bottom from cooking the steaks. Using the whisk, blend in the flour. Whisk until smooth.

Whisk in the milk. Add the salt, pepper, and onion powder. Whisk until it starts to boil. Boil and stir for 2 minutes.

YIELD:

4 servings

NUTRITION:

Nutrition Facts

Serving Size 211 g

Amount Per Serving	
Calories 291	Calories from Fat 145
	% Daily Value*
Total Fat 16.1g	25%
Saturated Fat 8.7g	44%
Cholesterol 79mg	26%
Sodium 1335mg	56%
Total Carbohydrates 12.2g	4%
Sugars 8.1g	
Protein 21.4g	
Vitamin A 25% •	Vitamin C 0%
Calcium 17% •	Iron 18%

High in iron.

High in calcium

NOTES:

Serve with the turkey ham.

TURKEY GIBLETS GRAVY

Turkey giblets gravy was a favorite gravy of mine when I was growing up. I love the flavor of the giblet meat and the addition of the boiled egg.

Taste before serving – don't be afraid of the seasonings. You want to serve a flavorful gravy.

INGREDIENTS:

1 turkey neck
1 set giblets, reserved from turkey
1 small onion
1 medium carrot
1 stalk celery
$^1/_4$ tsp salt (Kosher or sea salt is best)
6 cups water
1 tsp thyme
1 tsp rosemary
1 bay leaf
1 tsp whole black peppercorns
1 egg
2 TBS flour (I use fresh ground soft white wheat)

SUPPLIES:

Large saucepan
Small saucepan
Whisk
Measuring cups/spoons
Sharp knife/cutting board
Strainer

PREPARATION:

Roughly chop the onion ①, carrot, and celery.
Hard boil the egg ①.

DIRECTIONS:

Place the neck, giblets, vegetables, and spices in the saucepan. Bring to a boil. Reduce heat, cover, and simmer for about 30 minutes.

Strain the broth and return it to the saucepan, reserving about $^1/_2$ cup of the broth. Let that $^1/_2$ cup cool. Whisk the flour into the reserved broth until smooth. Bring the broth in the saucepan to a boil. Whisk in the flour/broth mixture. Continue to whisk as it comes back to a boil. Boil and stir for about 1 minute.

Chop the giblets and add the meat to the gravy. Chop the egg and gently stir it into the gravy.

Taste and check salt and pepper. Add more as taste needs.

YIELD:

8 servings

NUTRITION:

Nutrition Facts

Serving Size 220 g

Amount Per Serving

Calories 45	Calories from Fat 14
	% Daily Value*
Total Fat 1.6g	2%
Trans Fat 0.0g	
Cholesterol 35mg	12%
Sodium 108mg	5%
Total Carbohydrates 3.6g	1%
Dietary Fiber 0.7g	3%
Sugars 0.8g	
Protein 4.3g	

Vitamin A 36%	•	Vitamin C 3%
Calcium 3%	•	Iron 5%

High in iron

High in selenium

Very high in vitamin A

High in vitamin B12

NOTES:

Keep warm until ready to serve.

ⓘ Here are Hallee the Homemaker's instructions on how to hard boil an egg: http://www.halleethehomemaker.com/perfect-hard-boiled-egg/

ⓘ For information about a tip for chopping onions, follow this link: http://www.halleethehomemaker.com/chopping-veg/

TRADITIONAL TURKEY GRAVY

Turkey gravy is so vital to a turkey dinner. It is the final touch, and what could make or break the meal. It's also amazing poured over open faced turkey sandwiches. Don't be afraid of the seasonings – let the gravy be wonderful and full of flavor.

INGREDIENTS:

2 cups Tasty Turkey Broth (If you don't have any pre-made, you can use the juice from roasting your turkey. I have directions on my Hallee the Homemaker website to help you Roast the Perfect Turkey ①.)

$^1/_2$ tsp black pepper

1 tsp ground sage

2 tsp dried parsley

$^1/_4$ – $^1/_2$ tsp garlic powder (to taste)

$^1/_4$ – $^1/_2$ tsp onion powder (to taste)

salt to taste

3 TBS organic cornstarch

$^1/_2$ cup cool Tasty Turkey Broth ① or water

SUPPLIES:

saucepan

measuring cups/spoons

small bowl

Whisk

PREPARATION:

To make the turkey broth, you can remove the neck or a wing (or both!) from the turkey and cover with 3 cups of water. Add a roughly chopped carrot, a roughly chopped celery stalk, and about $^1/_4$ of an onion, about $^1/_2$ tsp salt. Bring it to a boil, then let it simmer for several hours (while the turkey cooks). Strain it when ready to make the gravy.

-OR-

Use the drippings from the pan from roasting your turkey.

-OR-

Refer to the Turkey Broth recipe in the front of this book or follow my recipe for Tasty Turkey Broth ⓘ on the Hallee the Homemaker website.

I've done it each way and don't have an end-result preference. Usually it depends on the quantity and whether I want to store some Tasty Turkey Broth for future use.

DIRECTIONS:

Bring 2 cups of broth, pepper, sage, parsley, onion powder, and garlic powder to a boil. (Note: depending on the flavor of your broth, you may not need all of these seasonings – taste it and determine that.)

In a small bowl, whisk the cold broth (or water) with the cornstarch until smooth.

Using a whisk, slowly pour the cornstarch mixture into the broth. As soon as it thickens, remove from heat (overcooking cornstarch will make it lose its thickening power.)
Salt to taste.

YIELD:

About 2 cups – or 8 servings

NUTRITION:

Nutrition Facts

Serving Size 37 g

Amount Per Serving

Calories 8	Calories from Fat 0
	% Daily Value*
Total Fat 0.0g	0%
Trans Fat 0.0g	
Cholesterol 0mg	0%
Sodium 171mg	7%
Total Carbohydrates 1.7g	1%
Protein 0.4g	

Vitamin A 0%	•	Vitamin C 0%
Calcium 0%	•	Iron 1%

* Based on a 2000 calorie diet

No saturated fat

No cholesterol

 NOTES:

Taste as you season. So many variables make broths have different levels of seasoning. Sometimes you need more spices, sometimes you need less. Don't be wary of spicing up a bland gravy - your family will thank you for it.

ⓘ You can find Hallee the Homemaker's instructions on how to roast the perfect turkey here:

http://www.halleethehomemaker.com/perfect-bird/

ⓘ Follow up your perfectly roasted turkey with instructions for Hallee the Homemaker's Tasty Turkey Broth:

http://www.halleethehomemaker.com/bird-broth/

MAKE-AHEAD TURKEY GRAVY

This gravy is made ahead and put in the refrigerator. That way, the cook is not scrambling to make gravy while holiday guests are waiting on their dinner.

INGREDIENTS:

$^1/_4$ cup unsalted butter
1 small onion
3 cups Tasty Turkey Broth ⓘ
$^3/_4$ cup cooking wine (Madeira) ⓘ
2 TBS organic cornstarch
$^1/_4$ cup water
$^1/_2$ cup turkey drippings
Salt and pepper to taste (Kosher or sea salt is best/fresh ground pepper is best)

SUPPLIES:

Skillet
Sharp knife/cutting board
Wooden spoon
Small bowl and whisk
Measuring cups/spoons

PREPARATION:

Finely chop the onion ⓘ.
In a small bowl, gently whisk the corn starch with the water until well mixed.

DIRECTIONS:

In the skillet, melt the butter over medium-high heat. Stir in the onion and sauté for 5 minutes.

Add the broth and bring to a boil. Add the wine. Gently boil for 10 minutes.

Slowly the cornstarch mixture to the boiling starch. Boil and stir for about 2 minutes, then reduce heat to low and cook for an addition 5 minutes.

Cool and store in the refrigerator in a tightly covered container.

When ready to serve, gently heat in a skillet over medium heat, whisking until smooth. Spoon $^1/_2$ cup of pan drippings from a roasted turkey and stir into the gravy. Taste and season with salt and pepper.

YIELD:

8 servings

NUTRITION:

Nutrition Facts	
Serving Size 145 g	

Amount Per Serving	
Calories 199	Calories from Fat 167
	% Daily Value*
Total Fat 18.5g	29%
Saturated Fat 7.4g	37%
Trans Fat 0.0g	
Cholesterol 28mg	9%
Sodium 414mg	17%
Total Carbohydrates 3.6g	1%
Sugars 0.9g	
Protein 1.0g	
Vitamin A 4%	Vitamin C 1%
Calcium 1%	Iron 2%

Low in sugar

NOTES:

Making ahead of time and storing in the fridge is not a requirement for making this recipe – it just makes serving a holiday meal one-step less hassle free.

ⓘ Follow up your perfectly roasted turkey with instructions for Hallee the Homemaker's Tasty Turkey Broth:
http://www.halleethehomemaker.com/bird-broth/

ⓘ For information about a tip for chopping onions, follow this link:
http://www.halleethehomemaker.com/chopping-veg/

ⓘ If you abstain from alcohol even in cooking, substitute a 100% pure white or dark grape juice (make sure there is no apple juice in it) along with one teaspoon of distilled vinegar to approximate the same flavor and properties while cooking.

RAVISHED ROASTED WHIPPED TURKEY WHITE WINE GRAVY

ROASTED TURKEY WHITE WINE GRAVY

This recipe is a wonderful addition to any turkey menu. The addition of the white wine gives it clean, delicious flavor.

 INGREDIENTS:

Drippings from roasting a turkey
1 cup dry white wine ⓘ
$^{1}/_{2}$ cup flour (I use fresh-ground soft white wheat)
3 cups Tasty Turkey Broth ⓘ
4 cups water
Kosher salt and fresh ground pepper to taste

 SUPPLIES:

Roasting pan or medium saucepan
Whisk
Measuring cups/spoons
Mesh strainer

 PREPARATION:

I have directions on my Hallee the Homemaker website to help you Roast the Perfect Turkey ⓘ and make your own Tasty Turkey Broth ⓘ.

 DIRECTIONS:

Remove the turkey from the roasting pan. Place the roasting pan on the stove across two burners (if using a pan that cannot be heated on the stove, scrape drippings and browned bits into a medium saucepan). Heat drippings over medium-high, scraping up browned bits, until thickened, about 10 minutes.

Stir in the wine. Cook, stirring constantly, until syrupy – about 5 minutes.

Gradually whisk in flour, and cook, whisking constantly, until well mixed, about 1 minute. Gradually add 1 cup broth; cook, whisking, until flour is a deep caramel color, 2 to 3 minutes.

Gradually stir in remaining turkey broth and 4 cups water. Bring to a simmer. Cook, stirring occasionally, until gravy reaches desired thickness, 10 to 15 minutes.

Strain gravy through a mesh strainer. Discard solids. Season generously with salt and pepper to taste.

YIELD:

8 servings

NUTRITION:

Nutrition Facts

Serving Size 297 g

Amount Per Serving

Calories 529	Calories from Fat 466
	% Daily Value*
Total Fat 51.7g	80%
Saturated Fat 15.2g	76%
Cholesterol 52mg	17%
Sodium 291mg	12%
Total Carbohydrates 7.1g	2%
Sugars 0.5g	
Protein 2.7g	

Vitamin A 0%	•	Vitamin C 0%
Calcium 1%	•	Iron 4%

Very low in sugar

NOTES:

White wine really helps turkey gravy have a wonderful, clean flavor. Don't hesitate to use it - the alcohol will cook out, and your dinner guests will wonder what makes your gravy so much better than theirs!

ⓘ You can find Hallee the Homemaker's instructions on how to roast the perfect turkey here:
http://www.halleethehomemaker.com/perfect-bird/

ⓘ Follow up your perfectly roasted turkey with instructions for Hallee the Homemaker's Tasty Turkey Broth:
http://www.halleethehomemaker.com/bird-broth/

ⓘ If you abstain from alcohol even in cooking, in that case you can substitute a 100% pure white or dark grape juice (make sure there is no apple juice in it) along with one teaspoon of distilled vinegar to approximate the same flavor and properties while cooking.

DARKER SHADES OF BEEF GRAVY

Beef is one of my favorite ingredients. You can slice it thin and make sandwiches, season it and grill it over open flame, put it in a pot with some root veggies and make a roast – it seems like the versatility of beef just goes on forever.

Ground beef is probably the harried housewife's best friend. Don't know what's for dinner? You can grab a pound of hamburger out of the freezer and just start cooking it, and decide what you want to do with it after it's cooked.

This second section of beef gravy recipes has some complex meals (Beef Short Ribs with Red Eye Gravy) and some *incredibly* easy recipes (Ground Beef Gravy with Mixed Vegetables).

It's a hodgepodge mixture of amazing gravies paired with delicious beef that will become your favorite section of this book.

GROUND BEEF GRAVY WITH MIXED VEGETABLES

This is a great recipe to have to make a quick meal. Serve it over potatoes or rice.

INGREDIENTS:

1 lb grass-fed ground beef
$\frac{1}{2}$ tsp salt (Kosher or sea salt is best)
$\frac{1}{2}$ tsp fresh ground pepper
1 medium onion
6 oz. Fresh mushrooms
1 TBS unsalted butter
$\frac{1}{4}$ cup flour (I use fresh ground soft white wheat)
2 cups beef broth
2 cups frozen mixed vegetables

SUPPLIES:

Skillet
Sharp knife/cutting board
Jar with a lid
Measuring cups/spoons

PREPARATION:

Dice the onion ①.
Slice the mushrooms.

DIRECTIONS:

Crumble the ground beef into the skillet. Season with salt and pepper. Heat on medium high heat until browned. Add the butter, onion, and the mushrooms. Cook until the onion is tender.

Mix the flour with the broth in the jar. Cover with lid and shake until smooth.

Pour into the pan with the meat mixture. Bring to a boil. Boil and stir for 1-2 minutes.

Add the vegetables. Cook until the vegetables are heated.

YIELD:

4 servings

NUTRITION:

Nutrition Facts

Serving Size 407 g

Amount Per Serving	
Calories 354	Calories from Fat 135
	% Daily Value*
Total Fat 15.0g	23%
Saturated Fat 6.6g	33%
Cholesterol 83mg	28%
Sodium 804mg	33%
Total Carbohydrates 22.5g	7%
Dietary Fiber 5.2g	21%
Sugars 5.1g	
Protein 30.6g	
Vitamin A 80% •	Vitamin C 10%
Calcium 6% •	Iron 30%

Very high in vitamin A

Very high in vitamin B6

NOTES:

Serve over mashed potatoes or rice.

ⓘ For Hallee the Homemaker's Wonderful Whipped Potatoes recipe, check out this link:
http://www.halleethehomemaker.com/whipped-potatoes/

ⓘ For Hallee the Homemaker's Perfect Brown Rice recipe, check out this link:
http://www.halleethehomemaker.com/brown-rice/

ⓘ For Hallee the Homemaker's Perfect White Rice recipe, check out this link:
http://www.halleethehomemaker.com/white-rice/

ⓘ For information about a tip for chopping onions, follow this link:
http://www.halleethehomemaker.com/chopping-veg/

OBSEQUIOUS ONION GRAVY BURGERS

ONION GRAVY BURGERS

With two boys, having a good recipe for onion gravy burgers will come in handy for many years. They are savory, delicious, and the make ground beef a beautiful thing.

INGREDIENTS:

1 pound grass fed ground beef

$^1/_2$ cup bread crumbs

1 envelope onion soup mix (read label and watch for MSG)

$^1/_4$ cup whole milk

1 egg

4 ounce can mushrooms (do not drain)

1 $^1/_2$ cup water

2 TBS flour (I use fresh-ground soft white wheat)

$^1/_4$ tsp dried basil

$^1/_4$ tsp dried oregano

$^1/_4$ tsp garlic powder

4 Hallee's Whole Wheat Hamburger Buns ⓘ

About 2 TBS butter

SUPPLIES:

Large bowl

Large, deep skillet with lid

Small bowl/whisk

PREPARATION:

Split each bun.

Spread each side with butter.

Toast buns in broiler.

DIRECTIONS:

Combine meat, crumbs, half of the package of onion soup mix, and egg until well blended. Shape into 8 patties, $^1/_2$ inch thick. Sauté in the skillet until browned on both sides.

In a small bowl, combine the remaining soup mix, mushrooms (with liquid), water, flour, herbs, and garlic powder. Mix with a whisk.

Pour over patties. Heat over high heat, stirring constantly, until boiling.

Reduce heat to low, cover and simmer, stirring occasionally, for 20 minutes.

Place each patty on a bun half, and top with gravy.

YIELD:

4 servings

NUTRITION:

Nutrition Facts

Serving Size 334 g

Amount Per Serving	
Calories 501	Calories from Fat 189
	% Daily Value*
Total Fat 21.0g	32%
Saturated Fat 9.4g	47%
Cholesterol 133mg	44%
Sodium 1303mg	54%
Total Carbohydrates 42.6g	14%
Dietary Fiber 2.8g	11%
Sugars 4.9g	
Protein 32.8g	
Vitamin A 5%	Vitamin C 1%
Calcium 15%	Iron 30%

High in iron.

High in calcium

NOTES:

I love to add a slice of Swiss cheese before slathering on the gravy. The flavors go together really nicely.

ⓘ For a recipe for Hallee's Whole Wheat Hamburger Buns, go to this address: http://www.halleethehomemaker.com/burger-buns/

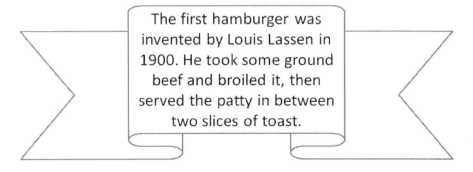

The first hamburger was invented by Louis Lassen in 1900. He took some ground beef and broiled it, then served the patty in between two slices of toast.

SALISBURY STEAK & ONION GRAVY

Salisbury steak and onion gravy is the perfect dish to make when you have some ground beef but just don't know what you want to do with it. It's a nice change from the regular chili mac casserole and is a from-days-old comfort food recipe.

INGREDIENTS:

$^1/_4$ cup extra virgin olive oil

1 large onion

2 slices bread

$^1/_2$ cup whole milk

2 pounds grass-fed ground beef

2 garlic cloves

1 large egg

2 TBS flat-leaf parsley

2 tsp plus a dash of Worcestershire sauce

Coarse salt (Kosher or sea salt is best) and freshly ground black pepper

1 tsp organic cornstarch, plus $^1/_4$ cup for dusting

1 $^1/_2$ cups beef broth

SUPPLIES:

Sharp knife/cutting board

Cheese grater

Small bowl for soaking bread in milk.

Large bowl.

Skillet

Measuring cups/spoons

PREPARATION:

Grate the onion (for a total of 1 $^1/_3$ cup onions).

Mince the garlic.

Chop the parsley.

Soak bread in the milk.

DIRECTIONS:

Heat a medium sauté pan over medium heat. Add 2 tablespoons oil and all but $^1/_3$ cup of the onion. Reduce heat to medium-low, and cook, stirring occasionally, until onions are golden brown and caramelized, about 35 minutes. Set aside.

Chop up the soaked bread. In a large bowl, combine the remaining $^1/_3$ cup onions, the ground beef, garlic, bread/milk, egg, parsley, 2 tsp Worcestershire sauce, 2 tsp salt, and $\frac{1}{4}$ tsp pepper. Mix with your hands to combine.

Divide meat mixture into 6 patties. Dust with cornstarch.

Heat a large skillet over medium-high heat. Add remaining oil and reduce heat to medium. Cook patties, 3 at a time, for 6 minutes on one side, and another 9 minutes on the other. Set aside on a plate. Repeat with remaining patties.

Make the gravy: Add cooked onions and 1 teaspoon cornstarch to same skillet, and stir for 1 minute. Raise heat to medium-high. Pour in broth and a dash of Worcestershire sauce, and whisk until broth is clear and slightly thickened, about 3 minutes. Remove pan from heat, and return patties and juices to skillet, spooning sauce on top.

 YIELD:

6 servings

NUTRITION:

Nutrition Facts

Serving Size 287 g

Amount Per Serving

Calories 417	Calories from Fat 226
	% Daily Value*
Total Fat 25.1g	39%
Saturated Fat 8.0g	40%
Trans Fat 0.0g	
Cholesterol 133mg	44%
Sodium 352mg	15%
Total Carbohydrates 11.1g	4%
Dietary Fiber 0.6g	2%
Sugars 2.8g	
Protein 34.3g	

Vitamin A 3%	•	Vitamin C 6%
Calcium 7%	•	Iron 23%

Low in sugar

High in Iron

 NOTES:

Serve over mashed potatoes or rice.

ⓘ For Hallee the Homemaker's Wonderful Whipped Potatoes recipe, go to: http://www.halleethehomemaker.com/whipped-potatoes/

ⓘ For Hallee the Homemaker's Perfect Brown Rice recipe, check out this link: http://www.halleethehomemaker.com/brown-rice/

ⓘ For Hallee the Homemaker's Perfect White Rice recipe, check out this link: http://www.halleethehomemaker.com/white-rice/

ROULADEN WITH GRAVY

Rouladen is a German dish. It is thinly sliced beef, rolled up with pickles and garlic. You think this won't work, until you taste it. Then you wish you'd doubled the recipe when you made it.

INGREDIENTS:

12 small thinly sliced steaks (tell your butcher it's for Rouladen)
6 tsp spicy brown mustard
2 large onions
1 dill pickle
2 TBS extra virgin olive oil
1 large bay leaf
2 small cloves garlic
$^1/_2$ cup organic cornstarch
Salt and pepper to taste (Kosher or sea salt is best/fresh ground pepper is best)

SUPPLIES:

Butter knife
Toothpicks
Sharp knife/cutting board
Large pot with lid
Wooden spoon

PREPARATION:

Finely dice the onions ①.
Dice dill pickle.
Spread each steak with $^1/_2$ tsp mustard. Sprinkle with onion and dill pickle. Sprinkle with salt and pepper.
Roll from the thin end and secure with a toothpick.

DIRECTIONS:

Heat extra virgin olive oil in the large pot over medium-high heat. Sear each meat roll on all sides. Remove from pan. Allow the drippings in the pan to brown.

Place the meat back into the pan. Add half of an inch of water. Mix the brownings in the pan with the water. Add the remaining onion, bay leaf, and cloves. Put the lid on and turn the heat to medium low. Heat until the meat is well cooked.

Remove the meat from the pan. Remove the bay leaf and cloves.

Mix cornstarch with $^{1}/_{2}$ cup cold water. Bring the water and drippings in the pan to a boil. Whisk in the cornstarch mixture. Boil for one minute, then reduce heat and simmer for about 10 minutes.

 YIELD:

6 servings

 NUTRITION:

Nutrition Facts

Serving Size 287 g

Amount Per Serving	
Calories 103	Calories from Fat 43
	% Daily Value*
Total Fat 4.8g	7%
Saturated Fat 0.7g	4%
Cholesterol 0mg	0%
Sodium 247mg	10%
Total Carbohydrates 15.0g	5%
Dietary Fiber 1.1g	4%
Sugars 2.2g	
Protein 0.7g	
Vitamin A 0% •	Vitamin C 7%
Calcium 1% •	Iron 1%

No cholesterol

 NOTES:

This is surprisingly good and has a great mix of flavors.

ⓘ For information about a tip for chopping onions, follow this link: http://www.halleethehomemaker.com/chopping-veg/

> Now behold, an angel of the Lord stood by him, and a light shone in the prison; and he struck Peter on the side and raised him up, saying, "Arise quickly!"
> And his chains fell off his hands.
>
> Acts 12:7

BEATEN BEEF LIVER WITH OBEDIENT ONION GRAVY

BEEF LIVER WITH ONION GRAVY

Livers and onions ... something adults find so delicious and most children dread seeing on the menu. They are a favorite of my husband.

INGREDIENTS:

2 lbs beef livers
$^1/_2$ cup unsalted butter, divided
$^1/_4$ cup flour (I use fresh ground soft white wheat)
2 tsp garlic powder, divided
1 $^1/_2$ tsp salt (Kosher or sea salt is best), divided
3/4 tsp fresh ground black pepper, divided
2 medium onions
2 cups beef stock
1 tsp paprika
$^1/_4$ tsp hot sauce
1 TBS organic cornstarch
$^1/_3$ cup filtered water

SUPPLIES:

Broiler pan
Skillet
Sharp knife/cutting board
Measuring cups/spoons
Baking dish
Foil

PREPARATION:

Slice the onions
Slice the liver

DIRECTIONS:

Sprinkle the liver slices with 1 tsp salt. $^1/_2$ tsp black pepper, and 1 tsp garlic powder. Toss with flour. Place on broiler pan. Top with pats of butter (4 TBS).

Broil until lightly browned. Turn and broil until lightly browned.

In the skillet, mix the beef stock, 4 TBS butter, $^1/_2$ tsp salt, $^1/_4$ tsp black pepper, hot sauce, and onion. Bring to a boil. Reduce heat and simmer until the onions are tender.

Mix cornstarch with $^1/_3$ cup water. Whisk into the broth mixture. Return to a boil. Boil and stir until thickened.

Heat oven to 325° F (150 ° C)

Place liver in baking dish. Pour gravy mixture over top. Cover tightly with foil and bake for 30 minutes.

YIELD:

6 servings

NUTRITION:

Nutrition Facts

Serving Size 310 g

Amount Per Serving	
Calories 449	Calories from Fat 205
	% Daily Value*
Total Fat 22.8g	35%
Saturated Fat 12.1g	61%
Trans Fat 0.3g	
Cholesterol 617mg	206%
Sodium 1076mg	45%
Total Carbohydrates 17.5g	6%
Dietary Fiber 1.1g	4%
Sugars 1.8g	
Protein 42.3g	
Vitamin A 802% •	Vitamin C 7%
Calcium 3% •	Iron 55%

Low in sugar

High in iron

Very high in niacin

Very high in pantothenic acid

High in phosphorus

Very high in riboflavin

High in selenium

Very high in vitamin A

High in vitamin B6

Very high in vitamin B12

High in zinc

NOTES:

Serve over mashed potatoes ①.

① For Hallee the Homemaker's Wonderful Whipped Potatoes recipe, check out this link:
http://www.halleethehomemaker.com/whipped-potatoes/

RAVISHING ESCULENT "RED" EYE GRAVY

RED EYE GRAVY

Red eye gravy, also known as poor man's gravy or bottom sop, is traditionally made with a fatty piece of country ham. We don't eat pork so my Red Eye Gravy is made with beef bacon grease. That works for me.

INGREDIENTS:

2 TBS beef bacon grease
$^3/_4$ cup strong brewed coffee
1 tsp brown sugar

SUPPLIES:

Skillet
Measuring spoons
Wooden spoon

PREPARATION:

Brew the coffee

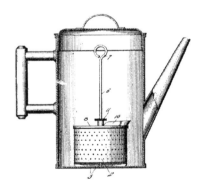

DIRECTIONS:

Melt the grease in the skillet over medium high heat. Add the coffee and the sugar. Bring to a boil.

Boil for 5 minutes. Serve.

YIELD:

4 servings

NUTRITION:

Nutrition Facts

Serving Size 7 g

Amount Per Serving

Calories 61	Calories from Fat 58
	% Daily Value*
Total Fat 6.4g	10%
Saturated Fat 3.2g	16%
Cholesterol 7mg	2%
Sodium 0mg	0%
Total Carbohydrates 0.7g	0%
Sugars 0.7g	
Protein 0.0g	
Vitamin A 0% • Vitamin C 0%	
Calcium 0% • Iron 0%	

Very low in sodium

NOTES:

Serve over grits ①.

① You can find Hallee the Homemaker's recipe for Southern Style Cheese Grits here:

http://www.halleethehomemaker.com/cheesey-grits/

SERVILE BEEF SHORT RIBS WITH WHIMPERING "RED" WINE
ROUGH & RED-EYE GRAVY

BEEF SHORT RIBS WITH RED WINE  RED-EYE GRAVY

This dish is unbelievably good. It is full of flavor and the perfect "company is coming" dish – especially if you're looking for a break away from a standard lasagna dish. The meat is falling off the bones and the gravy is absolutely succulent. It takes time, and preplanning, though.

INGREDIENTS:
3 cups fresh basil leaves and small sprigs
15 garlic cloves
$^3/_4$ cup extra virgin olive oil, divided
8 pounds meaty beef short ribs, cut crosswise across the bone
2 tsp Kosher salt (Kosher or sea salt is best)
2 tsp cayenne pepper
2 tsp paprika
2 tsp freshly ground black pepper
1 tsp chili powder
1 tsp dry mustard
1 TBS + $^1/_2$ tsp ground cumin, divided
$^1/_2$ tsp ground coriander
4 large onions
4 jalapeños ①
1 pound plum tomatoes, chopped
2 cups dry red wine ①
4 cups strong brewed coffee
3 cups chicken stock
3 bay leaves
$^1/_4$ cup red wine vinegar
3 TBS tomato paste
Salt (Kosher or sea salt is best) and freshly ground pepper to taste

**SUPPLIES:**
Food processor
Roasting pan or cast-iron casserole dish
Sharp knife/cutting board
Whisk, tongs, wooden spoon
Sharp knife/cutting board
Measuring cups/spoons

PREPARATION:

Halve the garlic cloves.

In a food processor, puree the basil and garlic. With the machine on, slowly add the $^1/_2$ cup extra virgin olive oil until blended.

Arrange the ribs in a large roasting pan and pour the basil marinade over them. Turn the ribs to coat them. Cover and refrigerate overnight.

Bring to room temperature before cooking.

Chop the onions ① and plum tomatoes.

Remove the seeds and membranes from the jalapeños ① Thinly slice them.

Brew the coffee

DIRECTIONS:

Scrape most of the marinade off the ribs and reserve. Season the ribs with the Kosher salt, cayenne pepper, paprika, black pepper, chili powder, dry mustard, $^1/2$ tsp cumin, and coriander.

In the roasting pan or cast iron casserole, heat 2 TBS of the extra virgin olive oil. Add half of the ribs to the pan and cook over medium-high heat until browned, turning once – about 4 minutes per side. Transfer to a platter.

Repeat with the remaining extra virgin olive oil and ribs. Transfer to a platter.

Add the onions to the pan. Cook over low heat until softened – about 15 minutes.

Increase the heat to medium and cook, stirring occasionally, until browned – about 10 minutes longer. Add the jalapeños, 1 TBS cumin and the reserved marinade. Cook, stirring occasionally, until peppers are soft, about 5 minutes. Add the tomatoes and cook over medium high heat for 5 minutes. Add the wine and simmer for 3 minutes.

Add the coffee, chicken stock, and bay leaves. Return the ribs and any accumulated juices to the pan. Bring to a boil, cover, reduce heat, and simmer over low heat until very tender – about 2 hours. You will want to skim the fat from the surface occasionally.

Transfer the ribs to a platter and discard the bay leaves. Discard the bones and trim the ribs of excess fat, keeping the meat intact.

Boil the gravy over high heat, stirring, until reduced to 6 cups – about 12 minutes.

Whisk in the vinegar and tomato paste; season with salt and pepper. Add the meat to the gravy, cover and simmer for 5 minutes before serving.

YIELD:

6 servings

NUTRITION:

Nutrition Facts

Serving Size 1211 g

Amount Per Serving	
Calories 1,625	Calories from Fat 730
	% Daily Value*
Total Fat 81.1g	125%
Saturated Fat 24.6g	123%
Trans Fat 0.0g	
Cholesterol 550mg	183%
Sodium 1707mg	71%
Total Carbohydrates 23.0g	8%
Dietary Fiber 4.2g	17%
Sugars 9.5g	
Protein 179.1g	

Vitamin A 38%	•	Vitamin C 55%	
Calcium 21%	•	Iron 84%	

Low in sugar
High in niacin
Very high in selenium
High in vitamin B6
High in vitamin B12
High in zinc
High in Vitamin A
High in Vitamin C
High in Iron

NOTES:

Serve with grits or saffron rice.

ⓘ You can find Hallee the Homemaker's tips for handling hot peppers here: http://www.halleethehomemaker.com/tip-hot-peppers/

ⓘ You can find Hallee the Homemaker's recipe for Southern Style Cheese Grits here:
http://www.halleethehomemaker.com/cheesey-grits/

ⓘ For information about a tip for chopping onions, follow this link: http://www.halleethehomemaker.com/chopping-veg/

ⓘ If you abstain from alcohol even in cooking, in that case you can substitute a 100% pure white or dark grape juice (make sure there is no apple juice in it) along with one teaspoon of distilled vinegar to approximate the same flavor and properties while cooking.

CAPTIVATED CUBE STEAK IN RELUCTANT RED WINE GRAVY

CUBE STEAK IN RED WINE GRAVY

It's always wonderful to find a new "company's coming" meal. I love cube steak, and I love beef with sweet peppers. This is a delicious combination. Serving it with rice gives it the perfect flavor.

 INGREDIENTS:

For the Entrée:
4 grass fed beef cube steaks
2 TBS flour (I use fresh ground soft white wheat)
$1/4$ tsp oregano
$1/4$ tsp garlic powder
$1/2$ tsp salt (Kosher or sea salt is best)
2 TBS extra virgin olive oil

For the Gravy:
2 TBS flour
$1/3$ cup red wine ⓘ
4 oz fresh mushrooms
1 $1/4$ cup beef broth
1 green pepper
Small onion

 SUPPLIES:

Shallow dish for dredging steaks in flour
Deep skillet

 PREPARATION:

Slice green pepper into strips.
Slice onion.
Slice mushrooms.

 DIRECTIONS:

Heat oil in skillet over medium-high heat.

Sprinkle steak with oregano, garlic powder, and salt. Dredge in 2 TBS flour.

Cook steak in oil until browned on both sides. Remove.

Sprinkle 2 TBS flour into oil. Whisk until smooth. Add beef broth and wine. Stir constantly until mixture thickens and boils. Add onions, green pepper, and mushrooms. Return steak to pan.

Cover and cook over medium-low heat until vegetables are tender.

 YIELD:

4 servings

 NUTRITION:

Nutrition Facts

Serving Size 300 g

Amount Per Serving

Calories 430	Calories from Fat 261
	% Daily Value*
Total Fat 29.0g	45%
Saturated Fat 10.5g	53%
Cholesterol 60mg	20%
Sodium 961mg	40%
Total Carbohydrates 10.9g	4%
Dietary Fiber 1.4g	5%
Sugars 2.4g	
Protein 26.4g	
Vitamin A 2% •	Vitamin C 44%
Calcium 1% •	Iron 19%

High in vitamin B6

Low in sugar

 NOTES:

Serve over rice or noodles.

ⓘ For Hallee the Homemaker's Perfect Brown Rice recipe, check out this link: http://www.halleethehomemaker.com/brown-rice/

ⓘ For Hallee the Homemaker's Perfect White Rice recipe, check out this link: http://www.halleethehomemaker.com/white-rice/

ⓘ If you abstain from alcohol even in cooking, in that case you can substitute a 100% pure white or dark grape juice (make sure there is no apple juice in it) along with one teaspoon of distilled vinegar to approximate the same flavor and properties while cooking.

JUST A QUICKIE BEEF STROGANOFF

QUICK BEEF STROGANOFF

Beef stroganoff is my daughter's favorite meal. I like this recipe, because I can make it with ground beef. I don't have to simmer the beef to tender like I do in a traditional beef stroganoff – and the sour cream added to the end makes a lick-the-spoon good gravy.

INGREDIENTS:

1 lb grass-fed ground beef
$^1/_2$ tsp Kosher salt (Kosher or sea salt is best)
$^1/_2$ tsp fresh ground pepper
$^1/_2$ tsp garlic powder
1 medium onion
6 oz. fresh mushrooms
1 TBS unsalted butter
$^1/_4$ cup flour (I use fresh ground soft white wheat)
2 cups beef broth
1 cup sour cream or plain Greek yogurt

SUPPLIES:

Skillet
Sharp knife/cutting board
Jar with a lid
Measuring cups/spoons

PREPARATION:

Dice the onion ①.
Slice the mushrooms.

DIRECTIONS:

Crumble the ground beef into the skillet. Season with salt, pepper, and garlic powder. Heat on medium high heat until browned. Add the butter, onion, and the mushrooms. Cook until the onion is tender.

Mix the flour with the broth in the jar. Cover with lid and shake until smooth.

Pour into the pan with the meat mixture. Bring to a boil. Boil and stir for 1-2 minutes.

Remove from heat and stir in sour cream. Return to the heat and get it back to hot - but do not boil.

YIELD:

4-6 servings

NUTRITION:

Nutrition Facts

Serving Size 249 g

Amount Per Serving	
Calories 241	Calories from Fat 122
	% Daily Value*
Total Fat 13.6g	21%
Saturated Fat 6.7g	34%
Trans Fat 0.0g	
Cholesterol 65mg	22%
Sodium 538mg	22%
Total Carbohydrates 8.9g	3%
Dietary Fiber 0.8g	3%
Sugars 3.2g	
Protein 20.0g	
Vitamin A 4% •	Vitamin C 4%
Calcium 7% •	Iron 17%

Very high in vitamin B6

High in Iron

NOTES:

Serve over noodles or rice.

ⓘ For Hallee the Homemaker's Perfect Brown Rice recipe, check out this link: http://www.halleethehomemaker.com/brown-rice/

ⓘ For Hallee the Homemaker's Perfect White Rice recipe, check out this link: http://www.halleethehomemaker.com/white-rice/

ⓘ For information about a tip for chopping onions, follow this link: http://www.halleethehomemaker.com/chopping-veg/

"And now look, I free you this day
from the chains
that were on your hand."

Jeremiah 40:4

CLASSIC BEEF STROGANOFF

This is a wonderful company is coming dish – and my daughter's personal favorite. Serve it over rice or homemade noodles, and everyone will be happy with dinner.

 INGREDIENTS:

1 $^1/_2$ lbs grass-fed beef sirloin steak
8 ounces fresh mushrooms
2 medium onions
1 garlic clove
$^1/_4$ cup unsalted butter
1 $^1/_2$ cups beef broth
$^1/_2$ tsp salt
1 tsp Worcestershire sauce
$^1/_4$ cup flour (I use fresh-ground soft white wheat)
1 $^1/_2$ cups sour cream or plain Greek yogurt

 SUPPLIES:

Skillet
Wooden spoon
Measuring cups/spoons
Sharp knife/cutting board
Jar with lid

 PREPARATION:

Slice beef to $^1/_2$ inch thick slices.
Thinly slice the onions and the mushrooms.
Finely chop the garlic.

 DIRECTIONS:

In skillet over medium heat, cook mushrooms, onions and garlic. Remove from skillet and set aside.

Cook beef in same skillet until brown. Stir in 1 cup of the broth, the salt and Worcestershire sauce. Heat to boiling. Reduce heat. Cover and simmer 15 minutes.

In the jar, put remaining $^1/_2$ cup of the broth and the flour. Shake until smooth.

Stir into beef mixture. Add onion and mushroom mixture. Heat to boiling over high heat, stirring constantly. Boil and stir 1 minute.

Lower heat to medium. Stir in sour cream; heat until hot (do not boil).

YIELD:

6 servings

NUTRITION:

Nutrition Facts

Serving Size 321 g

Amount Per Serving	
Calories 456	Calories from Fat 241

	% Daily Value*
Total Fat 26.8g	41%
Saturated Fat 12.8g	64%
Trans Fat 0.0g	
Cholesterol 125mg	42%
Sodium 542mg	23%
Total Carbohydrates 11.5g	4%
Dietary Fiber 1.1g	5%
Sugars 4.8g	
Protein 40.7g	

Vitamin A 5%	•	Vitamin C 7%	
Calcium 8%	•	Iron 28%	

High in selenium

Very high in vitamin B6

High in vitamin B12

NOTES:

It is easier to slice raw beef when it is partially frozen.

Serve over noodles or rice.

ⓘ For Hallee the Homemaker's Perfect Brown Rice recipe, check out this link: http://www.halleethehomemaker.com/brown-rice/

ⓘ For Hallee the Homemaker's Perfect White Rice recipe, check out this link: http://www.halleethehomemaker.com/white-rice/

SAUCY CLUCKERS & CROWERS

Chicken is such a popular dish. You can bake it, roast it, broil it, grill it, boil it – it can be made into soups, stuffed into pies, or chubby little fingers can hold onto the leg and enjoy mama's fried chicken.

Often, though, chicken can be boring, or overcooked to dry. That is where these gravies come in. They will make a plain roasted chicken into the most fabulous meal of the week. A peppery country gravy will make your fried chicken the talk of the church potluck, and a savory smooth gravy will highlight the simplest roasted chicken.

Whichever recipe you want to make, don't be afraid of flavor. Season and spice and bring that poultry to life!

FRIED CHICKEN GRAVY

Fried chicken dinner would not be complete without a creamy, peppery, wonderful country gravy. This is such a great addition to the meal. This would also be great as a dipping sauce for fried chicken tenders.

INGREDIENTS:

2 TBS grease from making a batch of Southern Fried Chicken ⓘ

2 TBS flour (I use fresh ground soft white wheat)

1 cup whole milk

Salt and pepper to taste (Kosher or sea salt is best/fresh ground pepper is best)

SUPPLIES:

Skillet

Whisk

Measuring cups/spoons

PREPARATION:

Fry chicken. Remove from pan and discard all but 2 TBS of the grease.

DIRECTIONS:

Whisk the flour into the grease, scraping up all of the fried chicken bits from the bottom of the pan.

Whisk until smooth.

Slowly add the milk. Bring to a boil.

Boil and stir 1-2 minutes. Salt and pepper to taste.

YIELD:
4-6 servings

NUTRITION:

Nutrition Facts

Serving Size 48 g

Amount Per Serving	
Calories 74	Calories from Fat 51
	% Daily Value*
Total Fat 5.7g	9%
Saturated Fat 2.1g	10%
Trans Fat 0.2g	
Cholesterol 7mg	2%
Sodium 16mg	1%
Total Carbohydrates 3.8g	1%
Sugars 2.1g	
Protein 1.6g	
Vitamin A 1%	Vitamin C 0%
Calcium 5%	Iron 1%

Low in sodium

NOTES:

Serve over mashed potatoes.

ⓘ For Hallee the Homemaker's Wonderful Whipped Potatoes recipe, check out this link:

http://www.halleethehomemaker.com/whipped-potatoes/

ⓘ You can find Hallee the Homemaker's instructions for making a perfect batch of Southern Fried Chicken here:

http://www.halleethehomemaker.com/my-fried-chicken

A Father to those who have no father, a judge
of the widows, is God in his holy place.
Those who are without friends,
God puts in families;
He makes free those who are in chains;

Psalms 68:6-7[a]

PAPRIKA CHICKEN WITH SOUR CREAM GRAVY

It's always fun to try something a little different at dinner time. Paprika is a main ingredient in my fried chicken seasonings. Instead of a country gravy, a nice sour-cream based gravy makes this meal an amazing change from the typical fried chicken dish.

 INGREDIENTS:

1 cup buttermilk
1 tsp salt (Kosher or sea salt is best)
2 tsp paprika
1 tsp garlic powder
1 tsp fresh ground black pepper
1 tsp ground red pepper
$\frac{1}{2}$ cup + 2 TBS flour (I use fresh ground, soft white wheat)
4 chicken breasts (bone-in, skin-on)
$\frac{1}{4}$ cup extra virgin olive oil
2 TBS unsalted butter
$\frac{1}{2}$ cup evaporated milk
$\frac{1}{2}$ cup chicken stock
$\frac{1}{4}$ cup sliced green onion
8-ounces sour cream

 SUPPLIES:

Baker's cooling rack
Deep skillet
Sharp knife/cutting board
Measuring cups/spoons
Whisk
Wooden spoon

 PREPARATION:

Slice the green onion
Soak the chicken in buttermilk for at least 10 minutes.

DIRECTIONS:

Remove the chicken from the buttermilk and set on the baker's cooling rack.

Sprinkle with salt, garlic powder, paprika, and peppers. Dredge in $^1/_2$ cup flour.

Heat the oil in a large skillet over medium heat. Cook chicken 7 minutes on each side or until brown.

Remove the chicken from the pan. Add the butter to the pan. Whisk in the 2 TBS flour until smooth. Stir in the chicken broth and the evaporated milk. Heat to boiling, then boil and stir for 2 minutes. Add green onions.

Return the chicken to the pan. Reduce heat to low, cover, and cook for 10 minutes or until chicken is thoroughly cooked. Remove from heat.

Place chicken on serving platter. Stir sour cream into liquid in pan. Mix thoroughly. Pour over chicken.

YIELD:

4 servings

NUTRITION:

Nutrition Facts

Serving Size 315 g

Amount Per Serving	
Calories 682	Calories from Fat 396
	% Daily Value*
Total Fat 44.0g	68%
Saturated Fat 17.4g	87%
Cholesterol 179mg	60%
Sodium 909mg	38%
Total Carbohydrates 22.7g	8%
Dietary Fiber 1.4g	6%
Sugars 3.9g	
Protein 48.8g	
Vitamin A 30% •	Vitamin C 6%
Calcium 19% •	Iron 19%

Low in sugar

High in niacin

NOTES:

This is great served with spinach fettuccine

ROASTED CHICKEN GRAVY

When I fry chicken, I like to make a creamy country-style gravy. But, when I roast chicken, I like a flavorful gravy made with a broth instead of milk. This is so delicious and packed full of flavor.

INGREDIENTS:

Juices from roasting a chicken ⓘ plus enough chicken broth to make 2 cups
$^1/_2$ tsp black pepper
1 tsp ground sage
2 tsp dried parsley
$^1/_4 - ^1/_2$ tsp garlic powder (to taste)
$^1/_4 - ^1/_2$ tsp onion powder (to taste)
salt to taste
3 TBS organic cornstarch
$^1/_2$ cup cool chicken broth or water

SUPPLIES:

saucepan
measuring cups/spoons
small bowl
Whisk

DIRECTIONS:

Bring the juices/broth, pepper, sage, parsley, onion powder, and garlic powder to a boil. (Note: depending on the flavor of your broth, you may not need all of these seasonings – taste it and determine that.)

In a small bowl, whisk the cold broth (or water) with the cornstarch until smooth.

Using a whisk, slowly pour the cornstarch mixture into the broth. As soon as it thickens, remove from heat (overcooking cornstarch will make it lose its thickening power.)

YIELD:

About 2 cups – 8 servings

 NUTRITION:

Nutrition Facts

Serving Size 37 g

Amount Per Serving

Calories 8	Calories from Fat 0
	% Daily Value*
Total Fat 0.0g	**0%**
Trans Fat 0.0g	
Cholesterol 0mg	**0%**
Sodium 171mg	**7%**
Total Carbohydrates 1.7g	**1%**
Protein 0.4g	
Vitamin A 0% • Vitamin C 0%	
Calcium 0% • Iron 1%	
* Based on a 2000 calorie diet	

No saturated fat

No cholesterol

 NOTES:

NOTE: To make the chicken broth, you can remove the wings from the chicken and cover with 3 cups of water. Add a roughly chopped carrot, a roughly chopped celery stalk, and about $^1/_4$ of an onion, about $^1/_2$ tsp salt. Bring it to a boil, then let it simmer for several hours. Strain it when ready to make the gravy.

-OR-

Use the drippings from the pan from roasting your chicken. Taste as you season. So many variables make broths have different levels of seasoning. Sometimes you need more spices, sometimes you need less. Don't be wary of spicing up a bland gravy - your family will thank you for it.

ⓘ You can find Hallee the Homemaker's instructions for roasting a whole chicken here:

http://www.halleethehomemaker.com/perfect-chicken/

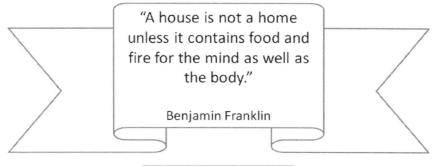

"A house is not a home unless it contains food and fire for the mind as well as the body."

Benjamin Franklin

QUICK & EASY CHICKEN GRAVY

This is a great recipe to have on hand for when you want a chicken gravy but don't have any drippings from roasting a chicken.

INGREDIENTS:

2 TBS unsalted butter

1 $^1/_2$ tsp extra virgin olive oil (or meat drippings)

$^1/_4$ onion

2 TBS flour (I use fresh ground soft white wheat)

1 $^1/_2$ cups chicken broth or water

2 tsp dried parsley

$^1/_2$ tsp onion powder

$^1/_4$ tsp dried sage

$^1/_4$ tsp dried thyme

$^1/_4$ tsp garlic powder (or 2 cloves minced garlic)

$^1/_4$ tsp fresh ground black pepper

1 $^1/_2$ TBS chicken soup base or bouillon (watch ingredients to avoid MSG)

SUPPLIES:

Sharp knife/cutting board

Skillet

Whisk

Measuring cups/spoons

PREPARATION:

Thinly slice or mince onion.

DIRECTIONS:

In skillet, melt butter over medium-high heat. Add the extra virgin olive oil or meat drippings. Add the onion (and the garlic if using fresh garlic). Cook until onion is tender. Whisk in the flour. Add the broth, seasonings, and soup base.

Bring to a boil over medium heat. Cook and stir for 2 minutes.

Reduce heat; simmer, uncovered, for 5 minutes.

YIELD:

6 servings

NUTRITION:

Nutrition Facts	
Serving Size 80 g	
Amount Per Serving	
Calories 66	Calories from Fat 48
	% Daily Value*
Total Fat 5.4g	8%
Saturated Fat 2.7g	14%
Cholesterol 10mg	3%
Sodium 1299mg	54%
Total Carbohydrates 3.0g	1%
Protein 1.6g	
Vitamin A 3% •	Vitamin C 2%
Calcium 1% •	Iron 2%

Low in sugar

NOTES:

① You can substitute $^1/_2$ cup of the cooking wine for broth . Let it simmer an additional 10 minutes if you're using the wine.

INVITING IDIOSYNCRATIC GRAVIES

This section is for all of the recipes that just didn't fit anywhere else. We have everything from lamb gravy to chocolate gravy.

The cool thing about an *a la carte* section is that it gives you some new ideas for some new recipes. When I'm thinking about what to make for dinner, a tuna gravy just isn't high on my brain's "go-to" list. But, once you make it, you'll want to come back again and again.

DOCILE AS A LAMB SLICK AS BUTTER GRAVY

LAMB BUTTER GRAVY

Lamb is a favorite meat in my house. It's nice to have a little change from a lamb stew or grilled lamb chops. This dish will be a new regular go-to for you. Serve it over saffron rice for a nice little kick.

INGREDIENTS:

2 pounds boneless lamb shoulder
$^1/_2$ tsp garam masala
1 tsp Kosher salt (Kosher or sea salt is best)
$^1/_2$ tsp fresh ground pepper
2 TBS unsalted butter
1 onion
1 clove garlic
$^1/_2$ tsp ground turmeric
$^1/_2$ tsp minced ginger
1 TBS tomato paste
$^1/_2$ tsp chili powder
1 cup water
$^1/_2$ cup crème fraîche
1 TBS honey
1 cup chopped fresh cilantro

SUPPLIES:

Sharp knife and cutting board (for meat and for veggies)
Measuring cups/spoons
Deep skillet
Wooden spoon

PREPARATION:

Cut the lamb into 1-inch pieces.
Dice the onion ①.
Mince the garlic.

PREPARATION:
DIRECTIONS:

Season the lamb with the garam masala, salt, and pepper. Heat 1 TBS of butter in the skillet over medium heat. Fry the lamb until browned, stirring occasionally. Remove from the skillet and set aside.

In the same skillet, add the remaining butter and cook over medium heat. When the butter is melted, stir in the onion and garlic. Add the turmeric and ginger.

Cook until the onion is tender.

Stir in the chili powder and tomato paste. Stir until well blended. Add the water.

Bring to a simmer and return the lamb back to the skillet. Cook, over low heat, until the lamb is tender.

Remove from heat and stir in the crème fraîche and honey.

Garnish with cilantro.

 YIELD:

6 servings

 NUTRITION:

Nutrition Facts

Serving Size 244 g

Amount Per Serving	
Calories 380	Calories from Fat 172
	% Daily Value*
Total Fat 19.1g	29%
Saturated Fat 8.9g	45%
Cholesterol 155mg	52%
Sodium 549mg	23%
Total Carbohydrates 6.6g	2%
Dietary Fiber 0.7g	3%
Sugars 4.1g	
Protein 43.6g	
Vitamin A 11%	• Vitamin C 5%
Calcium 5%	• Iron 22%

Very high in vitamin B12

Very high in selenium

High in niacin

High in zinc

 NOTES:

If you are looking for a quick meal, ground lamb would work wonderfully. Brown the ground lamb in the first step. When you return it to the pan, you only need to bring everything up to temperature, then serve it over rice.

Serve over rice.

Raw lamb is easier to slice when it is partially frozen.

ⓘ For Hallee the Homemaker's Perfect Brown Rice recipe, check out this link: http://www.halleethehomemaker.com/brown-rice/

ⓘ For Hallee the Homemaker's Perfect White Rice recipe, check out this link: http://www.halleethehomemaker.com/white-rice/

ⓘ For information about a tip for chopping onions, follow this link: http://www.halleethehomemaker.com/chopping-veg/

COERCED CREAMED TUNA TURNED ON TOAST

CREAMED TUNA ON TOAST

This is an age-old recipe for moms who need a quick, effortless meal. The creamy gravy with the high packed protein punch of the tuna and the delicious nutrition that comes with the addition of the peas – this is a great recipe. It's wonderful to make for a late supper, or when you're just too tired to worry about what to make for dinner. Serve it over toast.

 INGREDIENTS:

$^1/_4$ cup unsalted butter
$^1/_4$ cup flour (I use fresh ground soft white wheat)
2 cups whole milk
1 can solid white tuna in water
1 cup frozen peas
$^1/_2$ tsp salt (Kosher or sea salt is best)
$^1/_4$ tsp fresh ground pepper
8 slices bread

 SUPPLIES:

Skillet
Whisk
Measuring cups/spoons

 PREPARATION:

Toast bread.
Drain tuna.

 DIRECTIONS:

Melt the butter in the skillet over medium heat. Whisk in the flour until smooth. Slowly whisk in the milk.

Heat over medium heat until it thickens and boils. Cook for 2 minutes.

Stir in the salt, pepper, tuna, and peas. Heat through.

Serve over the toast.

 YIELD:

8 servings

NUTRITION:

Nutrition Facts	
Serving Size 123 g	
Amount Per Serving	
Calories 161	Calories from Fat 77
	% Daily Value*
Total Fat 8.5g	13%
Saturated Fat 5.0g	25%
Cholesterol 31mg	10%
Sodium 358mg	15%
Total Carbohydrates 13.2g	4%
Dietary Fiber 1.5g	6%
Sugars 4.5g	
Protein 8.4g	
Vitamin A 13% •	Vitamin C 3%
Calcium 9% •	Iron 6%

High in vitamin A.

High in Protein.

NOTES:

You can serve this over biscuits instead of bread.

ⓘ For Hallee the Homemaker's Whole Wheat Buttermilk Biscuits, check out this link:http://www.halleethehomemaker.com/buttermilk-biscuits/

HUMILIATINGLY QUICK & OBEDIENTLY EASY VEGETABLE GRAVY

QUICK & EASY VEGETABLE GRAVY

This is a simple gravy with clean, wonderful taste. It is a wonderful recipe to make to serve with a vegetarian meal. It also goes great with a fish or poultry meal. The mushrooms are such a great addition, and give it so much flavor.

INGREDIENTS:

2 TBS unsalted butter
1 $^1/_2$ tsp extra virgin olive oil (or meat drippings)
$^1/_4$ onion
6 oz fresh mushrooms
2 TBS flour (I use fresh ground soft white wheat)
1 $^1/_2$ cups vegetable broth or water
2 tsp dried parsley
$^1/_2$ tsp onion powder
$^1/_4$ tsp dried thyme
$^1/_4$ tsp garlic powder (or 2 cloves minced garlic)
$^1/_4$ tsp fresh ground black pepper
1 $^1/_2$ TBS vegetable soup base or bouillon (watch ingredients to avoid MSG)

SUPPLIES:

Sharp knife/cutting board
Skillet
Wooden spoon
Measuring cups/spoons

PREPARATION:

Thinly slice or mince onion.
Thinly slice mushrooms.

DIRECTIONS:

In skillet, melt butter over medium-high heat. Add the extra virgin olive oil or meat drippings. Add the onion and the mushrooms (and the garlic if using fresh garlic). Cook until onion is tender. Stir in the flour. Add the broth, seasonings, and soup base.

Bring to a boil over medium heat. Cook and stir for 2 minutes.

Reduce heat; simmer, uncovered, for 5 minutes.

YIELD:

6 servings

NUTRITION:

Nutrition Facts

Serving Size 127 g

Amount Per Serving	
Calories 79	Calories from Fat 49
	% Daily Value*
Total Fat 5.5g	8%
Saturated Fat 2.7g	14%
Trans Fat 0.0g	
Cholesterol 10mg	3%
Sodium 383mg	16%
Total Carbohydrates 5.2g	2%
Sugars 2.2g	
Protein 2.8g	

Vitamin A 3%	•	Vitamin C 3%
Calcium 1%	•	Iron 7%

High in niacin

Very high in vitamin B6

NOTES:

Serve over mashed potatoes or rice.

ⓘ For Hallee the Homemaker's Wonderful Whipped Potatoes recipe, check out this link:
http://www.halleethehomemaker.com/whipped-potatoes/

ⓘ For Hallee the Homemaker's Perfect Brown Rice recipe, check out this link:
http://www.halleethehomemaker.com/brown-rice/

ⓘ For Hallee the Homemaker's Perfect White Rice recipe, check out this link:
http://www.halleethehomemaker.com/white-rice/

CHAINED UP CHOCOLATE GRAVY

CHOCOLATE GRAVY

Chocolate and gravy …what could be better? This is really amazing served over biscuits ⓘ. Or, you know, just eaten with a spoon. You could even be totally naughty and use it as a dip for sugar cookies. Not that I've ever done anything like that…

INGREDIENTS:

$^1/_2$ cup sugar
$^1/_3$ cup unsweetened baking cocoa
$^1/_2$ cup flour (I use fresh ground soft white wheat)
1 cup whole milk
1 12-ounce can evaporated milk
1 egg
1 $^1/_2$ tsp vanilla extract ⓘ

SUPPLIES:

Saucepan
Small bowl
Measuring cups/spoons
Whisk

DIRECTIONS:

In a small bowl, mix the sugar, cocoa, egg, and $^1/_2$ cup of the whole milk.

In the saucepan, heat the remaining whole milk and evaporated milk. Over medium heat, heat to warm. Add the sugar/cocoa/egg/milk mixture.

Whisk as it heats to nearly boiling. Reduce heat to low and continue cooking until it reaches a pudding-like consistency.

It will thicken slightly as it cools.

YIELD:

2 $^1/_2$ cups – about 10 servings

NUTRITION:

Nutrition Facts	
Serving Size 82 g	
Amount Per Serving	
Calories 138	Calories from Fat 37
	% Daily Value*
Total Fat 4.1g	6%
Saturated Fat 2.4g	12%
Trans Fat 0.0g	
Cholesterol 29mg	10%
Sodium 52mg	2%
Total Carbohydrates 21.0g	7%
Dietary Fiber 1.2g	5%
Sugars 14.8g	
Protein 4.8g	
Vitamin A 3% •	Vitamin C 1%
Calcium 12% •	Iron 12%

Low in sodium

NOTES:

Serve over biscuits.

ⓘ For Hallee the Homemaker's Whole Wheat Buttermilk Biscuits, check out this link:
http://www.halleethehomemaker.com/buttermilk-biscuits/

ⓘ You can find Hallee the Homemaker's instructions on how to make super economical and incredibly delicious homemade vanilla extract, visit this link:
http://www.halleethehomemaker.com/homemade-vanilla/

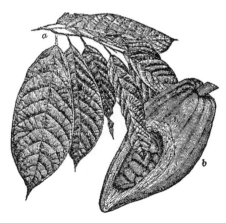

FIFTY SHADES GLUTEN FREED

Many recipes in this cookbook are gluten free, and you can find them by searching for the gluten free symbol. However, I went ahead and created a separate section and placed gluten free beef, turkey, chicken, and vegetarian gravy recipes in it for a quick and easy reference.

People with celiac disease or wheat allergies cannot eat products that contain gluten because it actually damages their intestines. There are also studies that show that gluten can create or enhance Attention Deficit Disorder (ADD) symptoms in children.

Gluten is the protein in wheat that gives dough its elasticity and helps the bread rise and keep its shape. The majority of recipes in this cookbook use flour as a thickening agent.

Gluten-free thickeners that can be used in gravies in lieu of flour are (organic) corn starch, chickpea flour (garbanzo beans), or rice flour. Those work wonderfully (though rice flour is sweeter - so taste as you're making) and can almost be substituted en-masse in these recipes. Don't be afraid to try gluten-free products to replace flour. You may stumble upon your new favorite gravy recipe.

GLUTEN FREE TURKEY GRAVY

When we have Thanksgiving with my brother's family, the entire meal is gluten free. This is a wonderful completion of a gluten-free turkey dinner. The rice flour thickens the gravy perfectly, and the addition of the wine gives it a wonderful flavor.

INGREDIENTS:

2 cups reserved pan juices from turkey roasting pan
2 TBS sweet rice flour
$1/2$ cup white wine ①
Salt and pepper to taste (Kosher or sea salt is best/fresh ground pepper is best)

SUPPLIES:

2-cup measuring cup or bowl
Skillet
Measuring cups/spoons
Whisk

PREPARATION:

Roast the Turkey ① Reserve 2 cups up the juices into a measuring cup or bowl. Use a spatula to scrape flavorful pan dripping into the cup or bowl.

DIRECTIONS:

When fat rises to the top of the cup, skim off $1/4$ cup of fat and pour into the skillet. Discard any remaining fat.

Mix rice flour with $1/2$ cup white wine. Stir until smooth and dissolved.

Add remaining pan juices to fat in the skillet. Whisk dissolved flour into the pan and cook over medium heat while continuing to whisk for about 5 minutes, until thickened. Add salt and pepper to taste.

YIELD:

2 cups

NUTRITION:

Nutrition Facts	
Serving Size 66 g	
Amount Per Serving	
Calories 473	Calories from Fat 460
	% Daily Value*
Total Fat 51.1g	79%
Saturated Fat 15.1g	75%
Cholesterol 52mg	17%
Sodium 1mg	0%
Total Carbohydrates 0.4g	0%
Protein 0.0g	
Vitamin A 0% •	Vitamin C 0%
Calcium 0% •	Iron 0%

Very low in sodium

Very low in sugar

NOTES:

You can use 2 TBS organic cornstarch in lieu of the rice flour.

ⓘ You can find Hallee the Homemaker's instructions on how to roast the perfect turkey here:
http://www.halleethehomemaker.com/perfect-bird/.

ⓘ If you abstain from alcohol even in cooking, in that case you can substitute a 100% pure white or dark grape juice (make sure there is no apple juice in it) along with one teaspoon of distilled vinegar to approximate the same flavor and properties while cooking.

GLUTEN FREE SAUSAGE GRAVY

Sausage gravy is a favorite in my region of the country – for breakfast or for dinner. My children love it and I add it to my weekly menu as often as possible. This is a wonderful gluten-free breakfast gravy recipe.

INGREDIENTS:

1 lb turkey breakfast sausage
1 small onion
1 TBS extra virgin olive oil
3 TBS unsalted butter
4 $^1/_2$ TBS organic cornstarch
3 cups milk
$^1/_2$ tsp salt (Kosher or sea salt is best)
$^1/_4$ tsp fresh ground black pepper

SUPPLIES:

Sharp knife/cutting board
Skillet
Wooden spoon
Measuring cups/spoons
Whisk

PREPARATION:

Finely mince the onion ①.

DIRECTIONS:

Heat the extra virgin olive oil in the skillet. Add the sausage and onion. Cook, stirring regularly, until browned. Remove from pan.

Reduce heat to low and place butter in pan. When butter is melted, whisk in the cornstarch until a thick paste is formed.

Increase heat to high and whisk in the milk, stirring constantly. When it starts to thicken, reduce the heat to medium.

Return the sausage mixture to the pan. Season with salt and pepper. Cook for an additional 2 minutes.

YIELD:

6 servings

NUTRITION:

Nutrition Facts

Serving Size 225 g

Amount Per Serving	
Calories 322	Calories from Fat 216
	% Daily Value*
Total Fat 24.0g	37%
Saturated Fat 5.5g	28%
Cholesterol 86mg	29%
Sodium 826mg	34%
Total Carbohydrates 12.3g	4%
Sugars 6.6g	
Protein 16.4g	
Vitamin A 4% •	Vitamin C 2%
Calcium 2% •	Iron 14%

Very high in vitamin B6

Very high in vitamin B12

NOTES:

Serve over gluten-free biscuits, potatoes, or rice.

ⓘ For Hallee the Homemaker's Family Fit Fried Potatoes recipe, check out this link:
http://www.halleethehomemaker.com/skillet-taters/

ⓘ For Hallee the Homemaker's Perfect Brown Rice recipe, check out this link:
http://www.halleethehomemaker.com/brown-rice/

ⓘ For Hallee the Homemaker's Perfect White Rice recipe, check out this link:
http://www.halleethehomemaker.com/white-rice/

ⓘ For information about a tip for chopping onions, follow this link:
http://www.halleethehomemaker.com/chopping-veg/

GLUTEN FREE VEGAN GRAVY

This is a wonderful addition to any gluten free meal. The chickpea flour is an awesome thickener, and gives it a punch of protein. The sage and thyme are a great flavor and will go with just about anything.

INGREDIENTS:

$^1/_4$ cup chickpea flour
$^1/_4$ cup extra virgin olive oil
2 cups vegetable broth
$^1/_2$ tsp dried thyme
$^1/_2$ tsp dried sage
$^1/_4$ tsp garlic powder
fresh ground black pepper to taste

SUPPLIES:

Saucepan
Whisk
Measuring cups/spoons

PREPARATION:

If you have a vegetable stock, make it into a broth.

DIRECTIONS:

In the saucepan over low heat, whisk together the extra virgin olive oil and chickpea flour. Whisk continuously for 8-10 minutes. Chickpea flour roux darkens faster than regular roux, so keep a close eye on it. Once it is as dark as you want it to be, remove from heat and let cool for 2-3 minutes.

Put the saucepan back on medium-low heat and add the sage, thyme, garlic powder, and pepper. Whisk to combine.

Slowly, $^1/_4$ cup at a time, pour the vegetable broth into the roux, whisking to combine.

Let the gravy simmer over medium-low heat for 20 more minutes, or until it is as thick as you want it.

YIELD:

6 servings

NUTRITION:

Nutrition Facts

Serving Size 98 g

Amount Per Serving	
Calories 116	Calories from Fat 84
	% Daily Value*
Total Fat 9.4g	14%
Saturated Fat 1.4g	7%
Cholesterol 0mg	0%
Sodium 256mg	11%
Total Carbohydrates 5.5g	2%
Dietary Fiber 1.5g	6%
Sugars 1.2g	
Protein 3.3g	
Vitamin A 0% • Vitamin C 1%	
Calcium 1% • Iron 5%	

No cholesterol

NOTES:

Serve over mashed potatoes or rice.

ⓘ For Hallee the Homemaker's Wonderful Whipped Potatoes recipe, check out this link:
http://www.halleethehomemaker.com/whipped-potatoes/

ⓘ For Hallee the Homemaker's Perfect Brown Rice recipe, check out this link:
http://www.halleethehomemaker.com/brown-rice/

ⓘ For Hallee the Homemaker's Perfect White Rice recipe, check out this link:
http://www.halleethehomemaker.com/white-rice/

GLUTEN FREE BEEF GRAVY

This is a wonderful addition to a gluten free meal. Cooking the spices and the vegetables in the beef stock just make what already is very flavorful an awesome flavor. It will go well with anything -from roast beef to steak to an open faced roast beef sandwich. This will be your new favorite beef gravy.

INGREDIENTS:

6 cups gluten-free beef stock

6 baby carrots

$^1/_2$ celery rib (with leaves)

1 small onion

4 medium fresh white mushrooms

2 small bay leaves

1 tsp dried parsley

1 pinch ground thyme

$^1/_2$ tsp garlic powder

$^1/_4$ tsp paprika

1 TBS gluten-free soy sauce

salt and pepper to taste (Kosher or sea salt is best/fresh ground pepper is best)

$^1/_4$ cup organic cornstarch

$^1/_2$ cup water

SUPPLIES:

Large saucepan with lid

Measuring cups/spoons

Sharp knife/cutting board

Fine mesh strainer

Food processor.

Small bowl

Whisk

PREPARATION:

Finely chop the onion ⓘ.

Quarter the mushrooms.

DIRECTIONS:

Place all ingredients except cornstarch and water in a large saucepan. Heat over high heat until it boils. Cover. Reduce heat to low and simmer for 1 hour.

Strain broth and remove bay leaves.

Place all the rest of veggies and herbs in a food processor and add enough broth to puree to a smooth consistency.

Pour both broth and puree back into pan, using a wooden spoon to deglaze the sides of the pan. Bring to a boil.

In a small bowl, mix together cornstarch and water. Stir till fully dissolved.

Whisk into boiling broth. Stir and boil for 1 minute.

Salt and pepper to taste.

YIELD:

8 servings

NUTRITION:

Nutrition Facts

Serving Size 58 g

Amount Per Serving	
Calories 87	Calories from Fat 1
	% Daily Value*
Total Fat 0.1g	0%
Trans Fat 0.0g	
Cholesterol 0mg	0%
Sodium 10477mg	437%
Total Carbohydrates 18.0g	6%
Dietary Fiber 0.7g	3%
Sugars 13.0g	
Protein 12.7g	

Vitamin A 22%	•	Vitamin C 3%
Calcium 1%	•	Iron 3%

Very low in saturated fat

No cholesterol

Very high in vitamin A

Very high in vitamin B6

NOTES:

Serve with roast beef dinner, over mashed potatoes or rice, or even in an open-faced roast beef sandwich (on gluten-free bread!)

ⓘ For Hallee the Homemaker's Wonderful Whipped Potatoes recipe, check out this link:
http://www.halleethehomemaker.com/whipped-potatoes/

ⓘ For Hallee the Homemaker's Perfect Brown Rice recipe, check out this link:
http://www.halleethehomemaker.com/brown-rice/

ⓘ For Hallee the Homemaker's Perfect White Rice recipe, check out this link:
http://www.halleethehomemaker.com/white-rice/

ⓘ For information about a tip for chopping onions, follow this link:
http://www.halleethehomemaker.com/chopping-veg/

THE STUFF IN THE REAR

AFTERWORD

By Hallee the Homemaker

1 Corinthians 10:31 reads, "Therefore, whether you eat or drink, or whatever you do, do all to the glory of God." I believe that applies to everything I do. Each time I prepare food for my family and serve it with love in my heart, I am doing so to the glory of God. Each time I consume anything in this fallen world, and anything that I produce, I am doing so for His glory. This principle includes my choice of movies, plays, or television shows I watch, music I listen to, and without question it applies to the books that I read and those I write.

For years now, I have been preparing recipes on my website with the intent of publishing my first cookbook. In all those years of preparing myself, I never imagined that my first cookbook would be about GRAVY, much less really quite good gravy recipes used to parody a really not so good fiction book.

I Peter 3:13 reads in part, "… be ready at any time when you are questioned about the hope which is in you, to make an answer in the fear of the Lord and without pride …" When a certain secular cultural phenomenon took over bookstore shelves, found space on the e-readers and coffee tables of friends and family members, and began to dominate my internet feeds, I felt restless with a desire to write my answer. My initial thought was a disbelieving cry of, "Oh good gravy! Even SHE read that horrible thing?"

Even though I wrote a few somewhat lengthy articles on the subject, I never published them. I had no desire to put anyone in my circle on the defensive about having read those specific very secular books, regardless of how pornographic and sinful they may be. Instead, I chose this comedic route. Parody the idea, even mock the tie on the book cover, and attempt to "redeem" it all.

So this cookbook is my answer to the secular cultural phenomenon that is a set of rather poorly written erotica books celebrating bondage, dominance, sadism, and masochism, which began as fan fiction for a rather silly young adult series about the undead. My answer to them is a good gravy cookbook intended to equip cooks all over the world with the ability to make virtuous, wholesome gravies and suitable sauces using whole food ingredients that ascribe to a Biblical diet.

I pray that you have fun with this book, that it gives you some tools and insight, and that you finish up amazing meals for your family and friends with the ultimate gravy or sauce. But I wanted to spend a few pages making an even more direct answer regarding that series of books this cookbook parodies and attempts to redeem.

First of all, dear reader, I haven't read them and don't plan to … ever. Nor will I ever see the inevitable trashy Hollywood film shortly to follow. I do not read erotic fiction and do not view pornographic portrayals. I have five reasons for this stance, and that is what I will share with you now.

First of all, I am convicted that they are sinful. The series of books is "erotic fiction". According to an erotic fiction website, the definition of erotic fiction is "writing that stimulates the senses". Jesus said, "You have heard that it said, 'Do not commit adultery.' But I tell you that anyone who looks at a woman lustfully has already committed adultery with her in his heart." (Matthew 5:27-28) I believe that is also true of a woman looking at – or reading about – a man and lusting. In short, according to Jesus, there is only one person who should ever stimulate sexual desire in me: my husband.

Secondly, to all the naysayers who say that I don't know because I haven't read them – the fact is that I do not have to read it or view it – or have any kind of personal, practical experience with it – to understand whether it will be good or bad for me. I do not have to be tied up and beaten know it would be painful and traumatizing. I do not have to drink poison to know it will make me sick and possibly kill me. I do not have to read those books – or see the film – to know they are sinful.

Third, I considered the cultural effect. Ever wonder why those books and their main theme are so wildly popular in our culture? This cookbook you are reading will help you make some really good gravy that is both healthy and delicious, and I don't think there is anything wrong with that. It seems like really good gravy would be a pretty popular idea. The other books not only misuse sex, but rather they redefine it into something evil as, from what I have learned, the lead male character first stalks in a very creepy way then utterly dominates the female lead in a consistently hurtful way. I think there is a lot wrong with that and it seems to me that it shouldn't be such a popular notion culturally speaking.

I believe, and have seen evidence again and again to support this, that in our often emasculating culture there is an unquenched hunger so great among women for strong men, decisive men, leading men, that women by the thousands will debase themselves and stoop to bondage, harsh dominance, sadism, and masochism to get even just a taste of the male strength they secretly crave. But God created men to be strong and lead so that men could provide and protect, not tie up and torture. God created women to be submissive to their own husbands (not anyone else's husband by the way) so that we could respect our husbands not for their excesses, but rather for their gentle and reserved restraint. God created sex to be the intimate glue to a partnership that's fueled by love and self-giving, not pain and humiliation.

We women were created to complete our men, to be loved and cherished as bone of his bone – flesh of his flesh – to become one with him. We were not created to be kidnapped, bound up, blindfolded, tormented, beaten, starved, terrorized, and punished. Likewise, men were not created to mentally and physically savage those physically weaker then them. Such evil should not be portrayed as good. Doing so is simply a lie.

Fourth, lust is not only hurtful to relationships but actually harmful to our physical bodies. Biopsychologists and other researchers who study the effects of lust, pornography, and erotica on the human brain and body all reach the same inescapable conclusion which is already available to us from wisdom which God gave us in His word thousands of years ago - "Flee sexual immorality. Every sin that a man does is outside the body, but he who commits sexual immorality sins against his own body." 1 Corinthians 6:18. Self stimulation and self gratification literally and physically damage our brains, and eventually we become less interested in real sex and more interested in self stimulation. Studies have shown that pornography, lust, and erotica rewire our brain's rational, moral, and value systems and make the brain addicted to the sexual stimulation. It is as addictive as drugs.

The Apostle Paul talked of putting on the full armor of God "to stand against the wiles of the devil (Ephesians 6:11)." And yet, when it comes to sexual immorality, idolatry, and greed, we are to run. To flee. We are not strong enough to stand against these things, so we are to remove them from our lives.

Reason number five is all the hype. It is exactly because of all the over-the-top hype that I chose to mock those books so specifically. Okay, I'm a mommy. I once overheard, while sitting in the bleachers of my kid's volleyball game, those other books described as really good "mommy porn." I tried to imagine a group of dads sitting in those bleachers laughing and joking about some really good "daddy porn" they had just enjoyed and had to wonder about how low our culture, and feminine womanhood, has sunk.

Hopefully, along with some good gravy ideas, I have given you some food for thought. I sincerely pray that God blesses you and grants you peace that passes understanding.

In Christ,

Hallee the Homemaker

MEASUREMENTS & CONVERSIONS

Liquid (Volume) Measurements (Approximate)				
1/3 TBS	1/6 fl oz	1 tsp	5 cc	5 ml
1 TBS	1/2 fl oz	3 tsp	15 cc	15 ml
2 TBS	1 fl oz	1/8 cup	6 tsp	30 ml
1/4 cup	2 fl oz	4 TBS	12 tsp	59 ml
1/3 cup	2 2/3 fl oz	5 TBS & 1 tsp	16 tsp	79 ml
1/2 cup	4 fl oz	8 TBS	24 tsp	118 ml
2/3 cup	5 1/3 fl oz	10 TBS & 2 tsp	32 tsp	158 ml
3/4 cup	6 fl oz	12 TBS	36 tsp	177 ml
7/8 cup	7 fl oz	14 TBS	42 tsp	207 ml
1 cup	8 fl oz	1/2 pt	16 TBS	237 ml
1 pt	16 fl oz	1 pt	32 TBS	473 ml
2 cups	16 fl oz	1 pt	32 TBS	473 ml
2 pts	32 fl oz	1 qt	1/4 gal	946 ml 0.946 l
4 cups	32 fl oz	1 qt	1/4 gal	946 ml
8 pts	1 gal/ 128 fl oz	4 qts	1 gal	3785 ml 3.78 l
4 qts	1 gal/128 fl oz	8 pts	1 gal	3785 ml 3.78 l
1 l	1.057 qts			1000 ml
1 gal	qts	128 fl oz		3785 ml 3.78 l

Dry (Weight) Measurements (approx)		
1 oz		30 g (28.35 g)
2 oz		55 g
3 oz		85 g
4 oz	1/4 lbs	125 g
8 oz	1/2 lbs	240 g
12 oz	3/4 lbs	375 g
16 oz	1 lbs	454 g
32 oz	2 lbs	907 g
1/4 lbs	4 oz	125 g
1/2 lbs	8 oz	240 g
3/4 lbs	12 oz	375 g
1 lbs	16 oz	454 g
2 lbs	32 oz	907 g
1 k	2.2 lbs/ 35.2 oz	1000 g

(DRY)	1 pt	0.551 l
	1 qt	1.101 l
	1 peck	8.81 l
	1 bushel	35.25 l

(WEIGHT)	1 oz	28.35 g
	1 lbs	453.59 g
	1 lbs	0.454 kg

(LENGTH)	1 in	25.4 ml
	1 in	2.54 cm
	1 ft	304.8 ml
	1 ft	30.48 cm
	1 yd	914.4 ml
	1 yd	91.44 cm

ABOUT THE AUTHOR

HALLEE BRIDGEMAN is a best-selling Christian author who writes action-packed romantic suspense focusing on true to life characters facing real world problems. Her work has been described as everything from refreshing to heart-stopping exciting.

An Army brat turned Floridian, Hallee finally settled in central Kentucky with her family so she could enjoy the beautiful changing seasons. She enjoys the roller- coaster ride thrills that life with a National Guard husband, a teenage daughter, and two elementary age sons delivers.

When not penning novels, she blogs about all things cooking and homemaking at Hallee the Homemaker™ (www.halleethehomemaker.com). Her passion for cooking spurred her to launch a whole food, real food "Parody" cookbook series. In addition to nutritious, Biblically grounded recipes, readers will find that each cookbook also confronts some controversial aspect of secular pop culture.

Hallee loves coffee, campy action movies, and regular date nights with her husband. Above all else, she loves God with all her heart, soul, mind, and strength; has been redeemed by the blood of Christ; and relies on the presence of the Holy Spirit. She prays her work here on earth is a blessing to you and would love to hear from you. Contact information is on her website.

COOKBOOKS BY HALLEE:

Fifty Shades of Gravy, a Christian gets Saucy

The Walking Bread, the Bread Will Rise

Iron Skillet Man, the Stark Truth about Pepper and Pots

FICTION BOOKS BY HALLEE:

Sapphire Ice, book 1 of the Jewel Series

Greater Than Rubies (a novella inspired by the Jewel Series)

Emerald Fire, book 2 of the Jewel Series

Topaz Heat, book 3 of the Jewel Series

Christmas Diamond (a novella inspired by the Jewel Series)

A Melody for James, book 1 of the Song of Suspense Series

An Aria for Nicholas, book 2 of the Song of Suspense Series

A Carol for Kent, book 3 of the Song of Suspense Series (upcoming)

HALLEE ONLINE

Hallee Newsletter
http://tinyurl.com/HalleeNews/

Never miss updates about upcoming releases, book signings, personal appearances, or other events. Sign up for Hallee's monthly newsletter.

Hallee the Homemaker blog
www.halleethehomemaker.com/

Hallee Bridgeman, Novelist blog
www.bridgemanfamily.com/hallee/

Better known as Bethlehem of Judea, the old Hebrew name *bêth lehem*, meaning "House of Bread," is known as the birthplace of King David and, above all, of Our Lord, Yeshua, known as Jesus of Nazareth. Thus, the "House of Bread" that is Bethlehem brought forth the Bread of Life that is our Savior.

The House of Bread Books™ imprint is pleased to publish healthy nutritious information in the form of cookbooks or informational pamphlets in order to better serve our community – the human race. We publish to reach every tribe and every nation for God has made of one blood all nations of men.

We pray that you enjoyed this fun attempt to redeem a recent secular phenomenon. Mostly, we pray that you come to know the joy and peace that is in serving Our Lord and Savior who is the King of kings, Lord of lords, and the Bread of Life.

Send inquiries to:

HOUSE OF BREAD BOOKS™
an imprint of: Olivia Kimbrell Press™
PO Box 4393
Winchester, KY 40392-4393

Or e-mail admin@oliviakimbrellpress.com

THE WALKING BREAD

While confronting and redeeming a recent popular secular phenomenon, Hallee Bridgeman, A.K.A. "Hallee the Homemaker" finds every grain of truth in her second whole food, real food cookbook with in-depth analysis and amazing recipes of yeast breads, quick breads, sourdoughs, and breads using grains other than wheat. The Walking Bread is a cookbook wrapped in a parody surrounded by a comedy with a tongue firmly inserted into a cheek -- but the recipes are "dead serious" and may leave readers searching for all the tasty bread crumbs.

> "I am the bread of life. Your fathers ate the manna in the wilderness, and are dead. This is the bread which comes down from heaven, that one may eat of it and not die. I am the living bread which came down from heaven. If anyone eats of this bread, he will live forever; and the bread that I shall give is My flesh, which I shall give for the life of the world." John 6:48-51

Readers, bakers, homemakers, and cooks all over the world will find themselves slathering the good stuff atop the muffins or corn bread; speeding through the quick breads; and going ape of over the banana bread. These bread recipes are so good, so healthy, and so easy you will want to pass them down from generation to generation.

Visit http://tinyurl.com/walkingbread for more slices of information.

IRON SKILLET MAN

It's a bird! It's a plane! It's a cookbook!

Move over men of steel! Make room mutants, aliens, and chemically or radioactively enhanced rescuers! Prepare to assemble your spatulas and get your "Flame on!" while the heroic Hallee the Homemaker™ (whose secret identity is Christian author and blogger Hallee Bridgeman) swings into action and shows her mettle with her third title in the Hallee's Galley parody cookbook series.

Is your skillet-sense is starting to tingle? Don't start crawling the walls, worthy citizen. Hallee constructs comic fun, jabbing at the cultural obsession with super powered heroes and villains. Along the way, readers will thrill to action packed explanations, daring "do it yourself" techniques, tremendous tips, and lots of real food/whole food recipes that achieve truly heroic heights. Ironically, while just a mild mannered cookbook by day, wrapped in a parody and surrounded by a comedy by night — the recipes are absolutely real and within the grasp of ordinary beings. Along with revealing the stark truth about pepper and pots, learn how to clean and season cast iron and care for cookware so it will last for generations. Recipes run the gamut from red meats to vegetables and from fish to fowl. Super skillet breads and divine desserts rush to the rescue.

In these colorful pages, you might just discover the x-factor to overcome even the most sinister kitchen confrontation. With Iron Skillet Man fighting for you, ordinary meals transform into extraordinary super powered provisions, whether cooking over a campfire or a conventional stove top.

Visit http://tinyurl.com/ironskilletman for more slices of information.

TABLE OF CONTENTS

Fifty Shades of Gravy

A

a la carte, 113
AU JUS, 3, 18, 19

B

BAKED MEATBALLS IN MUSHROOM GRAVY, 55
Beef, 82
beef bacon, 7, 25, 26, 47, 93
BEEF BACON GRAVY, 25, 26
beef broth, 6, 10, 12, 19, 21, 22, 27, 31, 35, 50, 51, 53, 58, 64, 83, 87, 98, 100, 102
BEEF GRAVY, 18, 23, 31, 35, 82, 83, 129
BEEF GRAVY MIX, 23
BEEF LIVER WITH ONION GRAVY, 91
beef plate, 25
Beef Short Ribs, 82, 95
BEEF SHORT RIBS WITH RED WINE RED-EYE GRAVY, 95
Beef stroganoff, 100, 102
Bible, 2, 4, 7, 8
BRAISED MEATBALLS IN RED-WINE GRAVY, 50
broth, 6, 9, 10, 11, 12, 13, 14, 15, 16, 17, 19, 21, 22, 27, 31, 35, 36, 45, 46, 50, 51, 53, 57, 58, 59, 64, 68, 73, 74, 75, 76, 78, 80, 83, 87, 88, 92, 98, 100, 102, 108, 109, 110, 111, 112, 118, 127, 130
butter, 6

C

Chicken, 104
chicken broth, 6, 14, 15, 45, 108, 109, 110, 111
chickpea flour, 122, 127
Chocolate, 1, 3, 113, 120
CHOCOLATE GRAVY, 120
Christ, 8, 134, 136
CLASSIC BEEF STROGANOFF, 102
Country fried steak, 37
COUNTRY FRIED STEAK & GRAVY, 37
country gravy, 37, 104, 105, 107

I

ITALIAN TOMATO GRAVY, 42

J

Jesus, 8, 133, 136

L

Lamb, 4, 49, 113, 114, 115
LAMB BUTTER GRAVY, 114
lamb shoulder, 114
legend, 4

M

MAKE-AHEAD TURKEY GRAVY, 78
Meatballs, 49
milk, 6, 23, 25, 29, 37, 38, 50, 51, 53, 55, 69, 71, 85, 87, 88, 105, 107, 108, 109, 116, 120, 125
monosodium glutamate, 6
MSG, 6, 23, 29, 31, 50, 62, 85, 111, 118
MUSHROOM GRAVY, 58
Mushrooms, 57

O

ONION GRAVY BURGERS, 85

P

PAPRIKA CHICKEN WITH SOUR CREAM GRAVY, 107
pork, 7

Q

QUICK & EASY BEEF GRAVY, 31
QUICK & EASY CHICKEN GRAVY, 111
QUICK & EASY HAMBURGER GRAVY, 27
QUICK & EASY VEGETABLE GRAVY, 118
QUICK BEEF STROGANOFF, 100

R

RED EYE GRAVY, 93
roast beef, 4, 19, 22, 31, 32, 35, 58, 129, 130
ROAST BEEF GRAVY, 35
ROASTED CHICKEN GRAVY, 109
ROASTED TURKEY WHITE WINE GRAVY, 80
ROULADEN WITH GRAVY, 89

S

S.O.S., 29
Salisbury steak, 87
SALISBURY STEAK & ONION GRAVY, 87
Sauce on a Slice, 29
Sausage gravy, 69, 125
sour-cream, 107
spaghetti sauce, 42
steak, 3, 18, 21, 22, 31, 33, 37, 38, 58, 87, 89, 98, 99, 102, 129
Steak Sauce, 18, 21, 22
stock, 6, 9, 10, 11, 12, 13, 14, 15, 16, 17, 18, 35, 60, 61, 91, 95, 96, 107, 127, 129
SWEDISH MEATBALLS & GRAVY, 53

T

TOMATO GRAVY, 47
tomatoes, 39
TRADITIONAL TURKEY GRAVY, 75
turkey, 66
turkey broth, 6, 16, 17, 75, 76, 78, 80
Turkey Cider Gravy, 67
TURKEY GIBLETS GRAVY, 73
TURKEY HAM GRAVY, 71
Turkey sausage, 42, 69
TURKEY SAWMILL GRAVY, 69

V

vegetable broth, 6, 10, 11, 45, 46, 118, 127
VEGETARIAN TOMATO GRAVY, 45

W

whole milk, 6
WILD MUSHROOM-SHALLOT GRAVY, 60
wine, 2, 5, 16, 18, 50, 51, 57, 59, 60, 66, 78, 80, 81, 95, 96, 98, 112, 123